Single but in a Relationship with God

Embrace the Single Season without Settling for Less than God's Best

Gabrielle Santiago

Trilogy Christian Publishers
A Wholly Owned Subsidiary of Trinity Broadcasting Network
2442 Michelle Drive
Tustin, CA 92780

For information, address Trilogy Christian Publishing
Rights Department, 2442 Michelle Drive, Tustin, Ca 92780.
Trilogy Christian Publishing/ TBN and colophon are trademarks of Trinity Broadcasting Network.

For information about special discounts for bulk purchases, please contact Trilogy Christian Publishing.

Manufactured in the United States of America

10 9 8 7 6 5 4 3 2 1

Library of Congress Cataloging-in-Publication Data is available.

ISBN 978-1-63769-038-3 (Print Book)
ISBN 978-1-63769-039-0 (ebook)

Dedication

To *Jesus*, who has been so merciful and never fails to show His love to me. I would not be where I am today if it weren't for Him

To *Michael*, my husband and my eagle, the man God made for me

To my *mom and dad* who have always been there for me through the good and the bad

Contents

Introduction

If you're picking up this book, you're most likely single. If you're not, don't put this book down because it can still help you. In this book, you will learn how being in a relationship with God will *change your life*. Maybe after reading this book, you'll realize that you're not ready for a relationship just yet or that you need to let go of the one you're currently in. If that's the case, you're about to experience one of the best days of your life.

I know being single sounds bad. It used to make me cringe when I told people I was single, but soon enough, I realized the beauty of being single. Even though I was single, I wasn't missing out because I was already experiencing the best relationship I could ever experience—a relationship with *God*.

Do you believe the single season can be one of the best times of your life? It can when you're living it with God. You will find in this book that your single season is one of the most important times of your life. It's the time for you to understand who you are and who God says you are. It's the time for you to be made whole, which can only happen through a relationship with God. If you leave your single season not fully ready and prepared, you are only setting yourself up for disaster. Rushing out of singleness is like forcing a butterfly out of its cocoon when it's not fully developed.

God wants to turn us into butterflies, and that happens through our time alone with Him. In our season of singleness, God is molding and equipping us to be unstoppable for the plans He has for us. He has amazing plans for each of our lives beyond what we can ever imagine.

> "What no eye has seen,
>   what no ear has heard,
> and what no human mind has conceived"—
>   the things God has prepared for those
> who love him—
>   1 Corinthians 2:9 (NIV)

You need to be prepared for what is coming. Embrace your cocoon phase with Jesus. This is the time when God will show you that He is all you need in life and that you can be satisfied in the *now*—not when you finally meet "the one" and get married. While all that is good, God wants you to realize that you were never created to chase after joy. Joy is found in Christ. He wants to show you that your relationship with Him is all you need and all-satisfying *today*.

I want you to finish this book feeling freed, encouraged, and ready to embrace singleness without settling for less than God's best. Are you ready to experience a relationship with a living God who will change your life? Are you ready to say with boldness, "I'm single but in a relationship with God"?

Who's Writing This Book Anyway?

If you don't know me already, you're probably wondering who I am. Before you read the rest of this book, you should probably know something about me and how I got where I am today.

You may think I have it all together because I run a ministry and a business, have an amazing husband, and wrote this book. If that's what's going on in your head, I want you to know that is totally *not* true.

First of all, I'm not perfect and was never perfect. For those who knew me way back in the day, you know *exactly* what I'm talking about. No one would have thought I would write a book about helping singles. Why? Because being single was my *greatest* fear.

I was known as the girl who *always* needed a boyfriend. On top of that, I was very shy and insecure. In high school, I was known as that quiet Asian girl—the one for whom the teacher had to make participation a grade because I would never raise my hand to speak.

My insecurity wasn't only in not being able to speak up; it was in every area of my life. I was insecure in the way I looked, in my ability to pursue my passions, and in my potential to go through life as a *single person.*

Because of my insecurities, I was always a dependent person. Growing up, I was very dependent on my parents. Unfortunately, unfaithfulness between my parents happened, which caused me to question my trust in them. The moment I realized I couldn't depend on my parents, I started looking elsewhere.

Where was the first place I looked?

Guys.

I grew up in a Christian household and went to church, but I never gave myself to Jesus or had a relationship with Him. It was no wonder I turned to guys for love and worth.

I started seeking self-worth and security from my first boyfriend. I thought he was all I needed. I told myself as long as he was with me, I'd be fine. He basically became *my everything*.

I couldn't make decisions on my own. Before I made any decision, I had to filter it through my boyfriend. I needed to be validated by his words. I needed him to say I was pretty in order to feel pretty. I needed him to say I was doing well so I would feel accomplished.

I thought being in a relationship would fix all my insecurities. I soon found, however, that putting myself in a relationship (when I clearly wasn't ready for one) only made my insecurities worse.

I became obsessive of my boyfriend. I needed to know where he was and what he was doing 24/7—no joke. I constantly feared he would cheat on me or leave me.

He had a past of going to strip clubs and watching pornography, which constantly made me question my self-worth. He would say that he had to learn to be satisfied with me, which made me feel not good enough.

On top of all that, he was ten years older than I was, and I was dating him behind my parents' back. I didn't feel happy being with him, but I thought he was all I had. I lost my virginity to this man when I never was ready to lose my virginity. I was just a junior in high school, a lost girl looking for love.

Unfortunately, at that time I was looking for love in the wrong places. He said things like, "If you love me, you will have sex with me." I wanted to prove my love for him, but deep inside I felt torn because I knew it was wrong. I knew I wasn't ready, but my desperation for love made me blind. I ended up giving everything I had for this man. At the age of 18, I left my home, family, and church to be with him.

After we were together a year, he asked me to marry him since he needed his green card to stay in the states. His visa was expiring. I was a citizen, which meant he could easily get a green card to stay in the states if we were married.

I wasn't even close to being ready for marriage. I was 19 and didn't have a clue what marriage meant and who was right for me. I found myself saying yes out of fear of losing him. Like I said before, he was all I had. I had left everything per his request. I couldn't take a chance of losing him.

So we went to the courthouse, got our marriage license, and got married. Three months later, he filed for his green card and got what he needed. That whole time no one but his family knew we got married.

Then things got worse. I wasn't able to visit my family per his family's request. He questioned me every time I visited my previous church friends. I felt so empty and alone, and on top of that, I felt bad for lying to everyone about my marriage.

I realized then that this man could never be my source of joy. This relationship became toxic to my spirit, soul, and mind. I thought being in a relationship would cure my insecurities, but it imprisoned me even more. I became subject to my own fears and insecurities.

Now that I look back, it's no wonder I was constantly afraid of losing my husband—he was my everything. I learned, however, that when you make something your everything (when it was never meant to be your everything), it ends up harming you.

Only Jesus can be your everything. I'll share more later on how I found that truth and how Jesus liberated me to a place of joy, peace, love, and freedom.

At the age of 20, I decided to divorce my husband. I was done being subjected to his rules and manipulations. Because so much was going on in my life, I felt drawn to go back to my home church where my parents attended. It was there that I met a new guy who caught my attention. Through my home church, I had more opportunities to hang out with this new guy. He encouraged me to seek God and move back with my family.

This should have been my time to remain single and focus on building a relationship with God, but I didn't. I still thought having a boyfriend was the solution to my problems and insecurities. This new guy then became my boyfriend.

I didn't tell anyone at that time about my previous marriage. I was afraid my parents would abandon me and this new guy wouldn't be interested in me, so I lived the lie for almost a year.

I felt horrible. I was being fake, but I convinced myself that this was the way I had to live. I told myself that I would always be in a deep pit, stuck with this shame.

Little did I know that there was actually a savior, Jesus Christ, who came to set us free from shame and darkness. Growing up, I always saw God as someone who would save us from eternal damnation but would never want to do life with me and give me life to the fullest. I didn't know that this Jesus could redeem every wrong I'd ever done and remove every shame I had hidden in my heart for years.

Later that year, I encountered that same Jesus at a conference called Passion where conviction hit me to confess my previous sins, especially about my previous marriage.

I was so scared. I came home debating whether I was ready to do this. It was in the hallway at my college that God finally spoke to me and said, "Then you will know the truth, and the truth will set you free" (John 8:32 NIV).

I was desperate. *I needed to be set free.* I had no other options but to take Jesus at His word and get my life right. I wasn't fully convinced that if I gave Him my all I would see His goodness, but He was the only option I had left for a chance to be set free.

That day in the hallway, I made the decision to give my life to Jesus and speak the truth to those who needed to know about my past. I was ready for my parents to abandon me and my new boyfriend to leave me. I was ready to lose everything for Jesus. I knew that if I wanted to experience all that Jesus had to offer, I had to give Him everything, even if it meant losing those I loved.

To my surprise, my parents and boyfriend accepted me even after I confessed my past. During that time, I learned about God's love. I truly understood that Jesus died on the cross to cleanse me from my sins. I learned that I could have hope and eternal life despite what I had done because of what Jesus did on the cross.

This was the start of my walk with God.

As I committed my life to God and took steps of faith, I started to see God real in my life. I spent every day in the Word, a time alone with God. I learned more about God and how to hear from Him. The more time I spent with God, the more my heart was being transformed. I started desiring what God desired. The more I experienced the revelation of His love, the more I wanted to give my life to Him.

If you're at the place where you feel completely lost with no hope, understand that Jesus is hope. He came to redeem the lost, to bind the brokenhearted, and to set captives free (Isaiah 61:1).

Give your life to Jesus, follow Him wherever He goes, and do whatever He tells you to do, and you will find freedom and life.

Going Deeper

God then put a burden on my heart to serve in the college ministry at my church and college. I had a heart for the lost because I had seen how God turned my life around when I was so lost. During this time, God also called me to share the gospel through writing, and I started a website, Living Revelations.

I wish I could say that from that point on my walk with God was good; however, I ended up slipping into impurity. My boyfriend started backsliding from God, and that caused me to fall into sexual sin. God told me I had to let go of this relationship because this guy wasn't the one for me. God also wanted to teach me that *only He could be my everything*.

God used my mentor and other confirmations to make it clear to me that my boyfriend wasn't the one to take me where I needed to go. But I still had not learned that only God could be my everything. I hadn't surrendered 100 percent to God. I had let go of many things, but there was still one last thing I couldn't lay down to God: *my boyfriend*.

I remember telling God, "You can have everything from my life, but don't touch my relationship." I was still depending on my boyfriend and *not God*. I tried convincing God that I could learn to trust in Him while still being in a relationship, but my *lack of obedience* proved that I was still subject to the fear of being single forever.

I disobeyed God and prolonged the relationship for a year and a half. During that time, my growth in God stopped. Why? Because there was no more I could grow. Whenever I spent my alone time with God, He told me the same thing— let go of the relationship.

I was like someone who wanted to get up to the calculus level but was not willing to pass the pre-calculus test first. God had a lot in store for me, but I first needed to learn to let go and pass this test so I could be ready for what He had in store for me.

I fought with God and made up excuses so He would allow me to stay in the relationship. I told God, "What if I could change him? What if I could make him love you?" What I failed to see during that time was that only Jesus can change lives. He's only willing to change hearts that *want* to be changed.

(Side note: For those who are in a relationship where you are trying to change the other person, it's best that you stop. You can't change them, and you will not change them. This will save you so much heartbreak.)

I finally reached a point of burnout. The more I tried to bring my boyfriend closer to God, the more bitter he became toward God. I realized that if I stayed in this relationship, I was jeopardizing my own future and the plans God had for me.

I knew deep inside that if I continued to disobey God, He would use someone else to continue His plans. I didn't want to miss out on what God had for me. He had given me big dreams and visions for my ministry, Living Revelations.

I knew I needed to be made whole and complete in Christ to get to the level of reaching the dreams God had put in my heart. God was trying to perfect me, and that could only happen during my season of singleness.

I finally decided to put my faith into action, and I broke off the relationship. It wasn't easy, and I didn't do it perfectly the first time. We broke up, and I entertained fears of being single forever. I allowed my fear to be greater than my faith and ended up back with him three months later. Six months passed, and things went back to square one. My boyfriend's relationship with God still hadn't changed, and I felt like my relationship with God was suffocating because of my boyfriend. It was then that I decided to officially break up with my boyfriend because I was finally convinced in my heart that *God knew better.*

The Start of My Single Season

I persevered through my season of singleness, understanding that God was *perfecting my weaknesses.*

> Because you know that the testing of your faith produces perseverance. Let perseverance finish its work so that you may be mature and complete, not lacking anything.
> James 1:3–4 (NIV)

The year I became single was the year I grew the most in the Lord. I was more sensitive to the voice of God, my confidence in Him was grounded, and doors of opportunities opened up.

I became one of the leaders in the singles ministry at church, and I had more speaking opportunities. My story and life encouraged many other singles who were struggling to let go of a relationship that wasn't of God.

My heart was to help singles understand the beauty of building a relationship with God and choose the right person to date (and eventually marry). God truly knew what He was doing when He asked me to let go of my boyfriend.

If you're holding on to a relationship that you know isn't right for you, I encourage you to let it go and trust God. Believe that God is good and faithful and that He knows better than you do. Just as God knew what was good for me, He knows what is best for you.

God wants to use your time of singleness to make you whole so you can be ready for what He has for you. Perseverance will prepare you to be *unstoppable* for the plans God has for you.

God made you and knew you before you were even born. He knows the plans for your life. *Will you trust Him?* "'For I know the plans I have for you,' declares the LORD, 'plans to prosper you and not to harm you, plans to give you hope and a future'" (Jeremiah 29:11 (NIV).

God has a good plan for you. Will you believe it?

God has a track record of never failing. We have the Bible so we can read stories of God's faithfulness. Everyone in the Bible who followed God's ways ended up prospering and being used mightily by God. When people in the Bible suffered, it was because of their own choice to disobey.

I have never regretted anything God has asked me to do. The regrets in my life are the times I did things my way and not God's way. Put your confidence in God, and you will see all the good promises He has for your life.

> So do not throw away your confidence; it will be richly rewarded. You need to persevere so that when you have done the will of God, you will receive what he has promised.
> Hebrews 10:35–36 (NIV)

Why would we choose to listen to our hearts when we don't have a perfect track record like God? We must understand that the human heart is deceitful (Jeremiah 17:9).

The only way to receive all of God's promises is by obeying Him and taking that step of faith. *What step of faith is God calling you to take?*

I'm writing this to testify to you that you can trust God. The best days of my life started when I obeyed God and entered into my single season. I struggled the first couple of months, but it was during those months that I learned to depend on God like never before.

I learned what it meant to meditate on his Word day and night. I found God's Word and promises to be food for my soul. It was the first time in my life that I really laid *all my life* down.

My only backup plan was God.

You know you've really surrendered to God when you have no backup plan. You don't have plan B to fall back on when things don't look good. Your only plan is to do whatever God tells you to do. Even when things don't feel right, you must continue to press on and trust His ways.

The moment I truly surrendered to God was when I found freedom in my life. The dreadful walk of singleness became a walk of *joy and adventure.*

I realized that I no longer had to walk in fear or bondage because my life was no longer in the hands of my boyfriend but in the hands of a *loving God*. I no longer had to worry about losing everything that mattered to me because God was my everything. He promises to never leave us or forsake us. "The LORD himself goes before you and will be with you; he will never leave you nor forsake you. Do not be afraid; do not be discouraged" (Deuteronomy 31:8 NIV).

When God becomes our everything, we no longer need to fear being alone because we are never alone. We don't have to be afraid if God will stop loving us because He will never stop loving us. In fact, there is no love greater than God's love. No person can love you as God loves you, and nothing can separate you from His love.

> For I am convinced that neither death nor life, neither angels nor demons, neither the present nor the future, nor any powers, neither height nor depth, nor anything else in all creation, will be able to separate us from the love of God that is in Christ Jesus our Lord.
> Romans 8:38–39 (NIV)

The Question That Showed Me I Changed

My turning point came when God asked me a question I thought I could never answer: "If you didn't have to be single, would you still be single for the sake of helping others?"

I remember choking up when I heard Him ask that. My instinct was to say no, but deep inside I knew that true joy was living in His will. If it was His will for me to be single, I would do it.

I said yes to God and cried that night. My tears were not of sorrow but of *joy*. If God had asked me that question a year ago, I would have said no in a heartbeat. He truly transformed my heart during my single season. I was completely *sold out to Jesus*.

At this point, I believed I was no longer in what I called my cocoon phase. I was a butterfly. The cocoon phase was the time for me to be alone (single) with God so He could do the work of maturity in me. As I got into my butterfly season, God was faithful and allowed me to get into a relationship with an amazing man whose heart truly sought after Jesus. Praise God I am now married to that man.

It still amazes me today to see that I am helping singles overcome the fear of singleness when I too was once one who struggled with that fear. We serve a God of miracles. He's able to take your greatest weakness and make it your greatest strength. God says in 2 Corinthians 12:9 (NIV), "My grace is sufficient for you, for my power is made perfect in weakness."

I was able to embrace my singleness and walk into an even greater season of life because I had developed a strong relationship with God. That's what this book is all about—to encourage you to enter into a *beautiful relationship with God*. God wants to make you whole and complete so your life will be a testimony to others. You don't need to wait to be in a relationship to experience true love and joy. *You can experience a greater love and joy right now with Jesus.*

It is by God's grace that I'm here today and writing this book to help you. Not only did I find the joy of being made whole in Christ, but since I surrendered my life to God, He has opened more doors to use me to help others. He's grown my territory of influence to help others who were just like me—lost and bound by fear.

The girl whose greatest fear was being single finally overcame it. No fear can hold her back anymore. That's a glimpse of my story. *Will this be your story, too?*

Why Are You Still Single?

Why are you still single? It's the question we all hate to hear. I heard this question at a singles conference at my church. The speaker, Kris Swiatocho, asked all of us, "Why are you still single?"

When I first heard this question, I thought to myself, *How is that answer going to help me?* But in that moment I realized that we all *should know* why we are single. I understand that not everyone is single because they aren't ready to be in a relationship, but that may be your reason.

Many times we blame God or pity ourselves for being single, but have we ever tried asking God and looking at our own weaknesses to see why God may still want us to be single?

There are many reasons why you may be single. It could be your own choice due to focusing on your career, or maybe you have fears from past relationships and are not ready to step into a new one. It could also be that you just haven't found the right person yet—and the list goes on.

While all of the above are valid reasons to be single, you may be single because *you're not ready for a relationship*. God may be asking you to be single because you haven't reached a level of maturity where you understand the point of being in a relationship. He still may want you to learn that He is all you need in order to be whole.

There are four main reasons why people want to be in a relationship.

1. Companionship
2. Security and stability
3. Fulfillment and purpose
4. Affection

If you want to be in a relationship because of any of these four reasons, you are *not ready* for a relationship.

Why? Because God never intended for our relationships or marriage to be for those four reasons. While spouses do play a part in fulfilling those four things, they should never be our main source. Our spouses were not created to fill us— *only God can fill us.* We can fill our spouses only because *God has filled us.* Think of God as the gasoline that will drive the car (our marriage) forward.

The mistake you can make is relying on your spouse too much and seeing him or her as our God. You will find yourself disappointed and dissatisfied. You can still feel lonely in the midst of a relationship or marriage. And no one can guarantee your security and stability. There is also no one like Jesus who can give you fulfillment and purpose that will leave you satisfied. Affection is not enough to keep a marriage intact.

Divorce rates have increased greatly because many people entered into marriage thinking a spouse would fill their emptiness. The reality is that *only God* can fill the emptiness that's inside of us and give us the desires of our hearts. Until we understand this, we are not ready to be in a relationship.

We may have the perception that a spouse is our better half to complete us, but God never said the halves will become one flesh. He said "the two will become one flesh"

(Mark 10:8 NIV). God wants us to learn that it is Christ who completes us. God's vision of marriage is *two complete people in Christ coming together to become one for a greater purpose for God's kingdom.*

The Purpose of Marriage

When we approach relationship with the mindset to be filled, we are setting ourselves up for disaster. Marriage was never created for our selfish desires. It was meant to help one another advance the kingdom of God here on earth.

Marriage isn't about what we can get from one another but what *we can give* to one another. It's a purifying process where we get to learn what it means to love someone unconditionally, just as Jesus loves us.

Here is God's command to wives: "Wives, submit yourselves to your own husbands as you do to the Lord" (Ephesians 5:22 NIV). And here's God's command to husbands: "Husbands, love your wives, just as Christ loved the church and gave himself up for her" (Ephesians 5:25 NIV).

If we want to know the purpose of marriage, we should go to the very first couple God created—Adam and Eve. Why did God create Eve for Adam? Because God knew Adam needed a helper. Genesis 2:18 (NIV) says, "It is not good for the man to be alone. I will make a helper suitable for him."

Adam was tasked by God to take care of the Garden of Eden and everything in it. Genesis 2:15 (NIV) says, "The LORD God took the man and put him in the Garden of Eden to work it and take care of it."

Just as Adam's duty was to take care of everything God gave him, God is also calling us to take care of the things He has given us in our lives. Whether it's our work life, family life, or ministry life, God has given us our spouse to help us accomplish His tasks.

The purpose of marriage is to be partners to build God's kingdom here on earth and to fulfill His purpose—to build what He has put in our hearts, to touch the lives of those around us, and to glorify God through it all.

When we lose the true purpose of marriage, it creates room for the enemy to attack our marriages. The reality is that there is a devil who is after our lives. He doesn't want us to experience God's realness and love, so he tries to distract us by persuading us to enter into relationships that were never meant for us.

If we want to see that God can meet all our needs, we have to first build a *relationship with Him.*

The Purpose of Your Relationship with God

The purpose of your relationship with God is to live out the reason God created you. You were created to know God intimately and to glorify Him in all you do. The only way to live the fulfilled life is to live the life you were created to live, which can only be done through a relationship with God.

As you build a relationship with God, you will see Him meeting all your needs and desires. A relationship with God is one that *can't be replaced.* There's no one on this earth who can give you what only God can give you.

Living life to the fullest comes from seeking Christ and not the things of this world. Jesus said in John 10:10 (NIV), "The thief comes only to steal and kill and destroy; I have come that they may have life, and have it to the full."

Having a relationship with a living and supernatural God is amazing. There's no one I have met who doesn't get excited when they experience a miracle or a supernatural touch of God. Those moments surpass our human understanding and scientific facts. Science can't define everything. Miracles do happen because there's a *real God* behind it all.

That real God calls you His child, and wants a relationship with you.

> For he chose us in him before the creation of the world to be holy and blameless in his sight. In love he predestined us for adoption to sonship through Jesus Christ, in accordance with his pleasure and will.
>
> Ephesians 1:4–5 (NIV)

This verse shows God's heart for us. Before God created the world, He desired for us to be holy and blameless in His sight. Because Adam and Eve (the first humans God created) disobeyed God and sinned, all humanity was birthed into sin (you can read more about Adam and Eve's sin in Genesis 3).

Our sin separates us from God because God is holy and cannot unite with those who are not holy. But because God loves us so much, He came to earth in human flesh through Jesus Christ and offered Himself as a sacrifice to redeem us from our sins. Jesus was the perfect sacrifice to wash away our sins forever. God did that so we could be together with Him for eternity in heaven.

1 John 1:7 (NIV) says that "the blood of Jesus, his Son, purifies us from all sin." Through Christ, we now can have a relationship with God the Father. He now lives in us and empowers us to live a righteous life for His glory.

Experiencing God's Love

Now that we understand the purpose of marriage and our relationship with God, it's time to see how applicable and real God's love for us can be. Just remember that *this book can never replace your actual relationship with God.* Knowing about God is different than experiencing a relationship with God. We can know everything about someone but not be in a relationship with them. Don't do that with God—He *wants* a relationship with you.

As we pursue a relationship with Jesus, we will find that He will never leave us thirsty. Jesus says in John 6:35 (NIV), "I am the bread of life. Whoever comes to me will never go hungry, and whoever believes in me will never be thirsty."

Once we've experienced a relationship with Jesus, we will never look for another person to fulfill our needs. Our marriage will never be one that looks to the other for love and fulfillment. It will be one that shares the overflow of love each person has experienced with God.

If we want to have a beautiful marriage that portrays a person who isn't in need but just gives, it starts with *a relationship with God.* It is crucial that we have a strong relationship with God before we pursue a relationship with another person.

It's only through a relationship with God that you can truly be changed and come to an understanding that God is your all. When God becomes your all, you never have to live in lack or in need. Everything you have is found in Him.

Make this psalm your proclamation.

The Lord is my shepherd, I lack nothing.
He makes me lie down in green pastures,
he leads me beside quiet waters,

he refreshes my soul.
He guides me along the right paths
for his name's sake.
Even though I walk
through the darkest valley,
I will fear no evil,
for you are with me;
your rod and your staff,
they comfort me.

You prepare a table before me
in the presence of my enemies.
You anoint my head with oil;
my cup overflows.
Surely your goodness and love will follow me
all the days of my life,
and I will dwell in the house of the LORD
forever.

Psalm 23 (NIV)

I covered a lot on marriage in this chapter because any relationship we get into should be with the intention of getting married. We must have a correct view of marriage before we enter into a relationship.

As you read the Bible, ask God to show you what marriage is in His eyes.

Here are some questions for you to reflect on.

1. Am I desiring a relationship because I'm afraid I'll grow old and alone?
2. Am I desiring a relationship because I need someone to help take care of me and my future family?

3. Am I desiring a relationship so I can be seen as valuable with purpose in my life?
4. Am I desiring a relationship so I can be fulfilled through experiencing romance and affection?

These questions will help you identify areas in your heart that need a revelation of who God is for you. Your spouse will play a part in meeting your needs, but your spouse is not the foundation. *Your help comes from God alone.*

I will cover in the next chapter how God can truly meet all your needs. The more surrendered you are to God, the better your relationship and marriage will be.

Ask God to show you why you are single and what He wants you to learn in this season.

Finding God's Love Real

We covered in the last chapter the four main reasons people want to be in a relationship:

1. Companionship
2. Security and stability
3. Fulfillment and purpose
4. Affection

Let's see now how God's love can be real and applicable in your life.

Companionship

One of the reasons you may want to be in a relationship is the fear of loneliness. No one wants to grow old alone, and the feeling of loneliness is never fun. Social media is great at making us feel empty when all we see are our friends constantly posting their engagement or marriage photos.

We can't help but feel left out. I remember how painful it was scrolling through social media and seeing most of my friends getting married. During that time, I was still with my boyfriend, but I knew God wanted me to let go of that relationship. I couldn't let go. The more I saw my friends getting married, the more scared I was of being left out and single.

I remember telling God, "I can't let him go. I don't want to miss out." But God's response to me was, "You're already missing out by holding on to him."

It was in that moment that I realized I *was* missing out. I realized I would never meet the right person if I kept holding on to the wrong person. I could have chosen to hold on to my boyfriend, but I would have missed out on God's best.

Are you holding on to someone you know you shouldn't be holding on to?

Many times we settle for less than God's best due to fear.

If only we knew that our fears are fake and that they are tactics the enemy uses to prevent us from experiencing God's best. I always thought, *Sure I'll meet a good Christian man, but what if I'm not attracted to him?* I found out later that I wasn't the only one who had this fear. I met plenty of other people who had the same fear. Many of us are afraid to let go because we're afraid we won't find someone better.

We end up talking ourselves out of the idea of breaking up due to the silliest fears. *What if I never meet someone I feel comfortable with? What if that person doesn't like the things I like? What if that person thinks I'm weird?*

If this is your first relationship, you might even be thinking, *What if I never meet anyone who loves me?* This was my fear during my first relationship, and I found out later that this was the silliest fear I held on to.

I'm sure there are plenty more what-ifs out there. The enemy is good at throwing fears at us to prevent us from letting go of what was never meant to be ours. But here's the truth: If God tells you to let them go, it's because He *does* have someone better for you.

I was able to learn this because I finally had the courage to let go of my boyfriend to eventually meet the one who was right for me. I never thought I would meet someone who could meet my needs both physically and spiritually, but I did. He was the person I had always prayed for. It was the first relationship where we both were growing closer to God and walking the same path in order to accomplish God's calling for our lives.

Before God walked me into this relationship, I first had to learn to be single and whole. I call this the cocoon season—the time when we get to be alone with God and become transformed into our new nature in Christ (the butterfly). I will talk about this more in later chapters.

Once again, I was able to testify that God knew best and was working for my good. I would never have been able to see God's faithfulness unless I had obeyed and broken off the relationship. Thankfully I did because I wouldn't be writing this book if I hadn't.

Are you holding on to someone and hoping they will change? Maybe they will change, but if God says they are not the one for you, that means they are not the best companion for you. God knows the best person for you because He created you. Trust His judgment and not your own.

We would have less stress in our lives if we just believed and did what God says. Many times we stress over our own decisions and try to control things that are clearly out of our control. Peace comes when we know we are in the will of God and have assurance in His goodness.

We have the choice to let God control our lives or to give our lives to the control of the enemy, who is the god of this world (2 Corinthians 4:4). Don't let the enemy fool you into thinking you have control of your life because you don't. Anything can happen, but when we submit our lives to God, we see His perfect, good, and pleasing will in our lives (Romans 12:2).

When we give God excuses to not obey Him, it shows that we don't trust that He knows best. Giving God excuses means we are still trying to control our lives.

If God has asked you to let go of someone, then let them go. Don't forget to also let go of your what-ifs. God knows all the what-ifs, and His only plan is to give you the best.

Knowing that God knows best sounds simple, yet it is difficult for many of us to believe. I know it was hard for me to believe, but ultimately, I had to make a simple choice to obey God. It was when I obeyed God that I saw the truth that God does truly know best.

As you let go of that person and walk into your single season, know that *the single life doesn't have to be a lonely life.* God is always with you, and He's always available to give you exactly what you need. The key is to look to Him first when you're in need.

Turn to God's Word, and He will speak to you and reveal truths to you. When you practice seeking God, you will start to hear Him more. James 4:8 (NIV) says, "Come near to God and he will come near to you."

I've found that when I've felt angry, sad, or doubtful, God has always spoken the right words to comfort me. I don't even have to go to my family or close friends for comfort because God has already healed my wounds. After I go to God and receive comfort, I then go to my loved ones and find joy in sharing with them my struggles and how God has helped me through them. Nothing can compare to the comfort and love of God's Word.

God is always available to hear your frustrations and speak truth in your situation. Here are some verses to encourage you as you go through a season where you may be feeling lonely.

> I will instruct you and teach you in the way you should go;
> I will counsel you with my loving eye on you.
>> Psalm 32:8 (NIV)

> But truly God has listened;
> he has attended to the voice of my prayer.

> Blessed be God,
> because he has not rejected my prayer
> or removed his steadfast love from me!
>> Psalm 66:19–20 (ESV)

God is able to love you when you feel unloved.

> The steadfast love of the LORD never ceases;
> his mercies never come to an end;
> they are new every morning;
> great is your faithfulness.
>> Lamentations 3:22–23 (NIV)

> Give thanks to the Lord, for he is good.
> *His love endures forever.*
>> Psalm 136:1 (NIV)

God is able to give you comfort when you're feeling sad.

> Praise be to the God and Father of our Lord Jesus Christ, the Father of compassion and the God of all comfort, who comforts us in all our troubles, so that we can comfort those in any trouble with the comfort we ourselves receive from God.
>
> 2 Corinthians 1:3–4 (NIV)

> The LORD is close to the brokenhearted
>   and saves those who are crushed in spirit.
>
> Psalm 34:18 (NIV)

God is able to give you peace when you're feeling scared.

> Do not be anxious about anything, but in every situation, by prayer and petition, with thanksgiving, present your requests to God. And the peace of God, which transcends all understanding, will guard your hearts and your minds in Christ Jesus.
>
> Philippians 4:6–7 (NIV)

The key to seeing these verses come alive in your life is to believe the very words of God as truth. Just as you are to take your friend's or loved ones advice, *take God's Word as truth*. Make God's Word the hope you hold on to, and you will eventually see the truth of God's Word become real in your life.

If you hold on to these verses and persevere, you will see that every word in the Bible is true. *It takes faith to see God as real in your life.* Faith is believing without seeing. Hebrews 11:1 (NIV) says, "Now faith is confidence in what we hope for and assurance about what we do not see."

Will you choose to run to God when you're feeling lonely and down? It's tempting to run to people or relationships when you're feeling lonely, but that will never fix your issue of loneliness. God is the only fix to loneliness. When you find God's presence to be ever so real in your life, loneliness will never be an issue. God is your best companion.

Security and Stability

Doing life is scary—bills that need to be paid, success we so desire to obtain, the future we want to build. All of it becomes daunting, especially when we have to go through it alone.

Security and stability were the main reasons I wanted to be in a relationship. I'm a very dependent person and have always needed someone to lean on. But God wanted me to learn that I only needed Him to lean on.

You're not alone in this journey of life—God is with you and for you. The desire for security and stability should never be the reason of your pursuit of a relationship. Why? Because no one on this earth can guarantee you 100 percent security and stability. *Only God can give us 100 percent assurance.*

God has a track record of never failing and always staying faithful. Deuteronomy 7:9 (NIV) says that "he is the faithful God, keeping his covenant of love to a thousand generations of those who love him and keep his commandments." We can be sure that we will have a prosperous life when we obey God.

God has never failed and will never fail. The Bible has thousands of promises that are guaranteed to be true to those who love Him. To love God means to put Him first before our feelings and desires. It means to follow God despite what we see and feel.

The great thing about following God is that we have 100 percent assurance that His ways are always the best for us.

> As for God, his way is perfect:
>> The LORD's word is flawless;
>> he shields all who take refuge in him.
> It is God who arms me with strength
>> and keeps my way secure.
>>> Psalm 18:30, 32 (NIV)

The word *perfect* means there's nothing better we can add. Your spouse will not add security to your life because your spouse doesn't know everything and doesn't have the power that God has. No one can surpass God's ability to take care of you.

God desires for you to be married, but not so your spouse can take over His job of taking care of you. God's ways will always lead us to a secure future. Ultimately, God is our provider. Yes, we may have great jobs and careers, but even those come from God. Every good gift comes from God (James 1:17).

Don't let the enemy lie to you and make you believe that God's ways are insecure. God's ways may feel insecure, but we must hold on to the truth that God is always for us.

God promises to give us life to the fullest, but it is the enemy who wants to pull us away from God's blessings. The enemy will use fear to stop us from pursuing God's will, but we must remember that only God's way brings us security. John 10:10 (NIV) reminds us, "The thief comes only to steal and kill and destroy; I have come that they may have life, and have it to the full."

Will you put your trust in God's faithfulness? Will you believe that God's ways are always good and secure no matter what you see or feel?

No job, person, or circumstance can guarantee you anything in life. You can only hold on to God's promises as truth and know He is faithful. Be confident that all your needs will be met when you surrender your life to God who loves you and wants to take care of you.

If you're looking for a place to rest, make God your home, and you will find rest. We're all looking for a place to rest after an exhausting day of school or work. We can run to God and make Him our safe haven.

> Whoever dwells in the shelter of the Most High
>   will rest in the shadow of the Almighty.
> I will say of the Lord, "He is my refuge and
> my fortress,
>   my God, in whom I trust."
>
> Psalm 91:1–2 (NIV)

If you're looking for help and protection, run to God because He wants to be your refuge and fortress—your home. Nowhere else can you get the rest that only God can give you. You will find rest when you make God your dwelling place. The beauty of depending on God is that *He will never fail you.*

God has never asked me to do anything I've later regretted. He truly will never fail you, and His faithful track record has been proved throughout the Bible.

The key to seeing God's faithfulness is through *our obedience*. If we are not willing to obey what God is telling us to do, we cannot expect to see God's faithfulness in our lives. He can only help those who are willing to turn to Him. The good news is that no matter how far we've run from God, He is always available with open arms for us.

Here are some verses to remind you that security and peace are always from God.

God's way is always secure and stable.

> It is God who arms me with strength
> and keeps my way secure.
> Psalm 18:32 (NIV)

> In all your ways submit to him,
> and he will make your paths straight.
> Proverbs 3:6 (NIV)

God's ways are always good.

> And we know that in all things God works for the good of those who love him, who have been called according to his purpose.
> Romans 8:28 (NIV)

> Surely your goodness and love will follow me
> all the days of my life,

and I will dwell in the house of the LORD
forever.
                              Psalm 23:6 (NIV)

And my God will meet all your needs according to the riches of his glory in Christ Jesus.
                         Philippians 4:19 (NIV)

God knows everything.

I am the Alpha and the Omega, the First and
the Last, the Beginning and the End.
                        Revelation 22:13 (NIV)

LORD, you have seen what is in my heart.
    You know all about me.
You know when I sit down and when I get up.
You know what I'm thinking even though
you are far away.
                        Psalm 139:1–2 (NIRV)

Look, God is greater than we can understand.
    His years cannot be counted.
                             Job 36:26 (NLT)

Although you may be single, know that you're not
alone. You have a mighty God who loves you and is for you.
He goes alongside you with power and glory. He knows all
things from the beginning to the end, so trust His ways.

Fulfillment and Purpose

We often look to our partner for fulfillment and purpose. We tend to find our identity in our relationships, but we must realize that no person can give us purpose. We should never place our identity in the hands of imperfect people—including our close loved ones.

Our identity becomes shaken when we place it in the hands of imperfect people. *When our identity is in the hands of a loving and perfect God, nothing can move us.*

Throughout my life, I always looked for validation and significance from what others said about me. I was a people-pleaser doing only things people told me to do.

Because my boyfriend was my most prized possession, I wanted to be what he wanted me to be. He was really into finance and always spoke highly of people who were successful in finance, so I strove for a finance career (even though I was a marketing major at the time). I didn't even consider the fact that I hated numbers. All that mattered to me was that I was becoming the person my boyfriend wanted me to be.

I did a pretty good job. During my senior year, I got a job offer as a financial consultant. I ended up getting another job offer as a marketing specialist at the company where I was an intern. It finally came time for me to choose which career path I would take. I was going to take the financial consultant position until I heard a sermon that changed my life.

The pastor encouraged people to focus on running in their own lane. He said the more you try to run in someone else's lane, the less likely you are to reach your own destination.

Focus on your lane.

At that moment I realized I was too busy looking at other people's lanes and not my own. *I was trying to pursue someone else's purpose while missing my own purpose.* I had forgotten I was made with purpose.

I also realized that even if I did pursue finance, I could never make my boyfriend proud because there would always be someone better than I was in finance. So why would I waste my time trying to pursue something I didn't even like and could never be the best at?

You can only be best at who you were created to be. Why? Because you were made for a unique purpose that no one else can do. Your purpose is found in God alone. We were not created to create our own purpose. We were created *with purpose.*

God says:

> Before I made you in your mother's womb, I chose you.
> Before you were born, I set you apart for a special work.
> Jeremiah 1:5 (NCV)

The key words in that verse are *special work.* God created you and chose you to complete a unique purpose here on earth—a work no one else can do but *you.*

The moment this revelation came to me, I started to seek God's purpose and will for my life. Choosing my career path was the first decision I ever made where I looked to God for guidance. Before that, I always followed what my parents or boyfriend suggested that I do. This job choice was one of the best decisions I made because it was a decision God made for me.

I prayed and sought God's will for which job offer to take. While the finance job did look more secure, I didn't feel at peace about it. During my prayer time with God, I heard these words: *Do not be afraid.* I instantly knew what He was referring to. I was afraid of pursuing my dreams to be a speaker and a writer.

I had secret desires to speak and become an author, but I thought it was a crazy thing to do. When I heard God speak those words, I knew what He was referring to.

That day, I chose to pursue God's calling and purpose in my life. I declined the financial consultant job and pursued the marketing job, which has helped immensely with what I am doing today. That day I took the first step toward my destiny.

Throughout the years, God has given me a clearer vision of what that purpose is. Fast forward to today. God has opened the door for me to speak and has given me the vision to start Living Revelations Ministries.

There's nothing more satisfying than living the life God created you to live. I could never experience this level of purpose and fulfillment in my life outside of doing God's will. Jesus said it Himself. "My food is to do the will of him who sent me and to accomplish his work" (John 4:34 ESV).

Here are some verses to encourage you on your journey to discover your calling and purpose from God.

God knows the plans for your life.

> "For I know the plans I have for you,"
> declares the LORD, "plans to prosper you and

not to harm you, plans to give you hope and
a future."

Jeremiah 29:11 (NIV)

Your eyes saw my unformed body;
    all the days ordained for me were writ-
ten in your book
    before one of them came to be.

Psalm 139:16 (NIV)

**God has great plans for your life beyond
what you can ever imagine.**

Now to him who is able to do immeasurably
more than all we ask or imagine, according to
his power that is at work within us.

Ephesians 3:20 (NIV)

"What no eye has seen,
    what no ear has heard,
and what no human mind has conceived"—
    the things God has prepared for those
who love him—

1 Corinthians 2:9 (NIV)

You are chosen and loved by God.

I took you from the ends of the earth,
    from its farthest corners I called you.
I said, "You are my servant";

45

I have chosen you and have not rejected
you.
Isaiah 41:9 (NIV)

So you are no longer a slave, but God's child;
and since you are his child, God has made
you also an heir.
Galatians 4:7 (NIV)

God has plans for your life. Seek your purpose in Him
and no one else. Your purpose and fulfillment are only found
in God because He created you.

Affection

We all long for affection. The first place we tend to look
for it is in a relationship. The problem is that affection alone
will never be enough. Without Jesus in the center of your life,
you will soon find that your significant other will never be
enough to satisfy you. There will always be an empty void in
you at the end of the day.

I'll use my friend as an example. He always told me
how he longed to be in a relationship. Physical touch was the
best way for him to feel loved. Unfortunately, he looked for
affection in the wrong places. He started seeking affection by
going on countless dates. Sure, he felt good during the dates.
He shared how holding their hand and feeling their touch
was the best feeling ever. But when the date was over and the
person was gone, he felt even emptier than before.

Can you relate?

He never took it as far as sex, but he always thought,
Maybe that would do it. Maybe you're at a place where you've

done those one-night stands and are living for the quick pleasures of life. How do you feel after them?

God never intended for us to chase after joy. He wants us to *live with joy.*

Seeking affection as a means to fill ourselves will only give us temporary happiness that will wear out and lead us to depression. We think seeking the affection of others will cure our depression, but it only makes it worse, and it can become addictive. The addiction doesn't apply only to sexual living; it even applies to seeking attention from others.

Throughout high school, I was constantly seeking the attention of guys. I was single and desperate for attention. I found myself getting caught up in calls and flirtatious texts with multiple guys to make myself feel better. Their attention was addictive, and I just couldn't stop.

Eventually when I started dating again, the attention I sought after was from my boyfriend. I am big on words of affirmation, so I was constantly seeking validation from him.

At one point, I wouldn't hear it enough from my boyfriend and thought, *Maybe he's not attracted to me.* Of course, it was all in my head.

I'm not saying that it's bad to look for affection from a significant other, but the source of our affection should never come from others. God should always be the source of all our needs and desires.

During my single season, I learned to find validation in God's Word alone. God's Word has all the validation we need.

Once you have a close enough relationship with God, you will also be able to hear Him speak over your life. While people can hurt us, God never can. We can always count on God and expect the best from Him.

I want to share the five love languages from Gary Chapman's book *The 5 Love Languages: The Secret to Love That Lasts.* Let's see how God displays all five love languages to us.

Physical Touch

Have you ever heard someone say, *I felt the presence of God*? You might be thinking, *How could they feel God's presence?*

Well, the reality is that God's presence is tangible. It's so tangible that some even fall down in His presence. Try being alone with God, and play some worship music. Start worshiping along with the music, and invite the Holy Spirit in. You will feel His presence over time.

Psalm 139:7 (NIV) says, "Where can I flee from your presence?" If God's presence is always with us, shouldn't we be able to feel His presence among us?

We are so quick to say that God doesn't speak or that we can't feel His presence, but what if it's just us not being sensitive enough to His presence? God will not barge into our lives uninvited. He's waiting for us to invite Him.

While physical touch from people lasts for a moment, God's touch lasts forever. Open your heart to God, and you will experience a touch like never before. You may not remember what God spoke to you that day or what the pastor preached, but you will always remember the touch of God you experienced.

Invite God, and tell Him you are desperate for His touch. Matthew 7:7 (NIV) says, "Ask and it will be given to you; seek and you will find; knock and the door will be opened to you."

Words of Affirmation

If you love words of affirmation, then you are going to love God because the Bible is filled with loving and encouraging words from God Himself. While the Bible was written by men, it is all God-breathed and inspired by God (2 Timothy 3:16).

God's Word can't compare to the words of others. His words are not just sweet sounding but are spirit and life—they have the power to transform and heal us.

Jesus said in John 6:63 (ESV), "The words that I have spoken to you are spirit and are life." While the words in the Bible alone are powerful, God wants to speak to you beyond what the verses say. He wants to make His words alive in your life.

What does it mean to see God's words alive in your life? It means that His words apply to whatever situation you may be facing. His words no longer are just written words on a page but are alive—healing and transforming your heart and soul.

Robert Crosby explains in his book *The One Jesus Loves* how the voice of God brings the Word of God to life. Crosby wrote, "It is the present Voice which makes the written Word all-powerful."[1]

---

[1] Robert Crosby, *The One Jesus Loves*, Nashville, TN: Thomas Nelson, 86.

God has every word of encouragement that will help you through any struggle you are facing. He yearns to speak life into your broken soul.

> Don't be afraid, for I am with you. Don't be discouraged, for I am your God. I will strengthen you and help you. I will hold you up with my victorious right hand.
>
> Isaiah 41:10 (NLT)

> In all these things we are more than conquerors through him who loved us.
>
> Romans 8:37 (NIV)

If you're feeling unloved, read the verses below.

> And I am convinced that nothing can ever separate us from God's love. Neither death nor life, neither angels nor demons, neither our fears for today nor our worries about tomorrow—not even the powers of hell can separate us from God's love. No power in the sky above or in the earth below—indeed, nothing in all creation will ever be able to separate us from the love of God that is revealed in Christ Jesus our Lord.
>
> Romans 8:38–39 (NLT)

> But God demonstrates his own love for us in this: While we were still sinners, Christ died for us.
>
> Romans 5:8 (NIV)

If you're feeling worthless, read the following verses.

> But you are a chosen people, a royal priest-
> hood, a holy nation, God's special possession,
> that you may declare the praises of him who
> called you out of darkness into his wonderful
> light.
>
> 1 Peter 2:9 (NIV)

> I praise you because I am fearfully and won-
> derfully made;
>> your works are wonderful,
>> I know that full well.
>
> Psalm 139:14 (NIV)

There are plenty more verses that will help you find comfort. Everything you need is found in God's Word.

I encourage you to write down verses that speak to you and keep them close to you. I like to keep a list of verses that encourage me and save them on my phone so I can reference them whenever I'm feeling down.

When I was going through my hardest breakup, I wrote promises that God had spoken to me along with verses that encouraged me on sticky notes and placed them on the walls of my room. I spoke God's truth over my life every day. Whenever doubt or fear crept into my mind, I instantly threw it out and replaced it with God's truth.

We can memorize and know a bunch of verses, but if we don't choose to believe them as truth, they will mean nothing. It's like someone telling you they love you, but you choose not to believe their words.

God's words mean nothing if we don't choose to believe them. We must be intentional in throwing away negative thoughts and replacing them with God's truth.

2 Corinthians 10:5 (NIV) reminds us to "demolish arguments and every pretension that sets itself up against the knowledge of God, and we take captive every thought to make it obedient to Christ." At the end of the day, we must also remember that God's words can't be compared to any-one else's words. Unlike others, God is 100 percent perfect, which means His words cannot be matched.

People's words may fail us, but God's words never will.

Acts of Service

If you feel most loved when people do things for you, that means your love language is acts of service. Just like the other love languages we covered, no one can beat God in acts of service. There's no other hand mightier than God's hands. We see throughout Scripture that it was through God's hands that people were saved.

When the Israelites were stuck in captivity under the strong hand of Pharaoh, it was God who saved them. Deuteronomy 26:8 (NIV) says, "So the LORD brought us out of Egypt with a mighty hand and an outstretched arm." God is all about showing off His glory. He will allow us to go through hardships so we can see His mighty hand do the impossible.

God wants to help you. Whether you need wisdom, instruction, favor, blessings, or an open door, God wants to help you with *everything*.

He can even help you in the workplace. I used to think God was only useful for ministry or church-related activities, but I soon found that He helped in every part of my life.

When I first started working, I tried to do things in my own strength and made silly mistakes. I forgot to do tasks I should have remembered to do and missed small details on my assigned projects.

I became stressed and worried before submitting a project. One day, it finally clicked. Why not ask God for help? I started praying over my projects and reviewing them with God before submitting anything to my manager. I prayed and asked God to show me anything that was missing or anything I could improve.

My work ethic improved to a point where my manager was very impressed. I went from doing a lot of rework to submitting projects and reports that needed no rework at all. God blessed my work as I sought Him for inspiration and wisdom in everything I did on my job.

I created presentations that became standards for coworkers to follow. I created systems and programs that were so successful that our first-year products got accepted in all doors when previously it would have taken three years for these products to be accepted in retail stores.

My company's CEO ended up categorizing me in the A team—people who were reliable and irreplaceable. As I sought God's help at work, He lifted me up and enabled me to be a true light.

Whether you're working or going to school, seek God for help. He will give you the strength and ability to succeed in all you do and have insights and ideas that will change the world.

James 4:2 (NIV) says, "You do not have because you do not ask God." When was the last time you asked God for help? Are you depending on Him for everything you have to do?

Here are some verses to help you find God's hand real in your life.

I will instruct you and teach you in the way
you should go; I will counsel you with my
loving eye on you.

Psalm 32:8 (NIV)

The LORD is near to all who call on him.

Psalm 145:18 (NIV)

With man this is impossible, but with God
all things are possible.

Matthew 19:26 (NIV)

Start asking God for help, and you will find His acts of
service are incomparable.

Gifts

We all love receiving gifts. The good news is that God is
a loving Father who loves blessing His children. James 1:17
(NIV) says, "Every good and perfect gift is from above, coming down from the Father of the heavenly lights."

Every good thing we have comes from God. Sure, other
people have played a part in giving you the things you have,
but it was God who used those people and placed you in
circumstances to receive those blessings.

When I was in college, I thought I would get a job by
practicing hard for my interviews. Don't get me wrong, you
do have to put in effort, work hard, and not expect things to
just be given to you.

But I found it funny that of all the hard interview
practices I did, I actually didn't practice at all for the job
I ended up getting. When I applied for my current job, I

didn't bother looking up the company or practicing too hard because I didn't want to work there anyway. It turned out that this company gave me a good offer, and I got the job. The other jobs I practiced so hard for did not accept me.

From this experience, God taught me that I can give my best, but ultimately, it is God who gives us what we have. I realized that every good gift I have comes from God. Even when my boyfriend gave me a gift, I gave thanks to God because I knew the money he had spent came from God.

I've also heard many of my friends tell how God provided for them supernaturally. One friend at the time was low on funds but wanted to have a piano at her new place. A month later, someone gives her a piano, and it was completely free.

That's the kind of God we have—one who gives extravagantly. No one can give like God because riches and wealth are all in His hands. Philippians 4:19 (NIV) says, "And my God will meet all your needs according to the riches of his glory in Christ Jesus."

Here are some verses to help you find God's hand real in your life.

> If you, then, though you are evil, know how to give good gifts to your children, how much more will your Father in heaven give good gifts to those who ask him!
> Matthew 7:11 (NIV)

> The LORD will command the blessing upon you in your barns and in all that you put your hand to, and He will bless you in the land which the LORD your God gives you.
> Deuteronomy 28:8 (NASB)

Remember, you have a Father in heaven who happens to be the best gift-giver.

Quality Time

If you long to spend quality time with someone, know that you can do just that with God. Although God may not be physically visible, He does speak.

We can actually have conversations with God. Many times we approach alone time with God and say to ourselves, *I hope God speaks to me today.* If you're giving God 30 minutes of your day, do you really think He won't speak to you?

God longs to talk to you. Many times we spend too much time talking in our prayers and not being still enough to wait and hear what He has to say. Often we rush through reading the Bible, trying to mark it off our to-do list. We don't realize that if we just lingered a bit longer, God would actually have something to say to us.

I see God's Word as conversation starters to hear God's voice. God's Word speaks life and is edifying, but many times God wants to speak to us beyond the words we read in the Bible and pour revelation into our minds.

Paul prayed for the people in Ephesus:

> I keep asking that the God of our Lord Jesus Christ, the glorious Father, may give you the Spirit of wisdom and revelation, so that you may know him better.
> Ephesians 1:17 (NIV)

My alone time with God started off lasting only 15 minutes, but when I slowly grew in my relationship with God, it went from 15 minutes to 30 minutes, and then to an hour. Now they can last up to 90 minutes and more.

I enjoy spending quality time with God because I get to interact with Him and hear what He has to say. Once you've tasted the joy of hearing from the almighty God and seeing Him open your eyes to insights and revelations, you will be excited to spend time with Him.

Invite God to speak, and make your prayer and alone time with God a two-way conversation. Ask God questions when you don't understand something in the Bible. Don't be afraid to ask Him to show you things. The key is to expect Him to answer.

Jesus has given us the Holy Spirit to guide us into all truth and guide us to scriptures we need. Here are some verses to help you find God real in your time with Him.

> But when he, the Spirit of truth, comes, he will guide you into all the truth. He will not speak on his own; he will speak only what he hears, and he will tell you what is yet to come.
>
> John 16:13 (NIV)

> Call to me and I will answer you and tell you great and unsearchable things you do not know.
>
> Jeremiah 33:3 (NIV)

May we all be like Samuel and respond to God like this: "Speak, for your servant is listening" (1 Samuel 3:10 NIV).

I hope you have learned in this chapter how God's love can be real in your life. While your significant other will play a role in loving you through the five love languages, you can still experience all of these love languages as a single person through a relationship with God.

You may be single, but you're definitely not missing out on experiencing the best love. No one can love you more than God.

First Love

Who do you think of when you hear the words *first love*? Maybe your first crush comes to mind. While you may have experienced the romantic butterflies in your stomach with whoever may have been your first love, there is a greater love. In this chapter, I'll talk about the creator of love who is also love Himself.

First, let's define what love is.

> Love is patient, love is kind. It does not envy, it does not boast, it is not proud. It does not dishonor others, it is not self-seeking, it is not easily angered, it keeps no record of wrongs. Love does not delight in evil but rejoices with the truth. It always protects, always trusts, always hopes, always perseveres. Love never fails.
>
> 1 Corinthians 13:4–8 (NIV)

We must also understand the source of love, which is God.

1 John 4:16 (NIV) says, "God is love," which means love originated from God. This is so important for us to understand because we are all seeking love, but many times God becomes our last resort for love.

We run to people and the things of this world to experience a love that only God can give. It's no wonder we find ourselves empty and not satisfied after seeking love from relationships or people.

If I had known that love comes from God, I would have saved myself from a lot of heartbreak with my previous boyfriends. I stayed in those relationships, even though they were no good for me, for the sake of experiencing love. I failed to see that love comes from God.

I'm not discrediting love that our loved ones give, but a *first love* must be experienced before we can enjoy the fullness of love from others. That *first love can only come from God.* Love that comes from God directly is called *first love* because it is God who created love.

If we have not experienced God's love, then we have not tasted the depths and power of what love can do. There is also no way we can love God if we haven't received His love into our lives.

1 John 4:19 (NIV) says, "We love because He first loved us." Love can never come from within us; it can only come from God.

God will never ask us to give anything He has not given us, which includes love. We must first experience His love in order to feel loved and to love God back.

Experiencing God's love is not a one-time experience; it's a continual growing experience. The more we grow in our relationship with God, the more we will experience the fullness of His love.

God's love never gets old. It's His love that fuels us to love the unlovable and feel love despite what our circumstances may be. We are all looking for love, but we must remember that love comes from God. Our pursuit of love should lead us to Jesus.

Looking for Love

Throughout my life, I was desperately seeking for love, but I looked for love in the wrong places and from the wrong people. I realized I couldn't find the love I was looking for from my parents, so I started looking into relationships.

I remember when I had my first boyfriend. I thought he was all I needed. I was even willing to lose friends and family to be with this guy, thinking that as long as he loved me, I would be okay. Of course, I soon found out that his love for me wasn't enough.

That's where we will all find ourselves when we try to find that first love from anyone other than God. If you're refusing to let go of a relationship or willing to lower your standards to just be in a relationship, then you are desperate for love.

But it's okay to be desperate for love. Why? Because God created us to be desperate for love but to be desperate for *His* love. It's our desperation for love that will take us deeper into our relationship with God. A desire and hunger to know God more stems from the love we so desire to experience from God.

Think about the last time you fell in love with someone. Didn't you want to know them more and spend all weekend with them? Pursuing a relationship with God is no different than pursuing a relationship with your loved one. It starts with the need for love and then includes the desire to give love.

As you develop a relationship with God, you will start to understand what true love is. Throughout the Bible are examples of God's unconditional love. You will also see how Jesus gave up His life so we could have eternal life with Him and live life to the fullest.

Jesus didn't wait until we had it all together to die on the cross for our sins. He died for us while we were yet sinners (Romans 5:8).

God's Love Pursues Us

No matter how determined we are to run from God, He is always pursuing us. I wouldn't be where I am today if it wasn't for His grace and mercy chasing after me. Yes, I had to make the choice to surrender my life to Him, but Jesus made a way for me to be made right before God by dying on the cross and rising from the grave.

When I was so far away and living apart from Him, He still pursued me and showed me that my past no longer can shame me. I love the book of Hosea where we can see God's love for us despite how bad we have been. In that book, God asks Hosea to marry Gomer, a promiscuous woman. Here's what God said to Hosea.

> Go, show your love to your wife again, though she is loved by another man and is an adulteress. Love her as the LORD loves the Israelites, though they turn to other gods and love the sacred raisin cakes.
>
> Hosea 3:1 (NIV)

God wanted to show His unconditional love for us through the life of Hosea in hopes that Israel (and we) would turn to Him.

> She will chase after her lovers but not catch them;

she will look for them but not find them.
Then she will say,
"I will go back to my husband as at first,
for then I was better off than now."

Hosea 2:7 (NIV)

We have a compassionate God whose love for us endures. No matter what you've done or how far you've been from God, He still wants you. God said this to Hosea:

My people are determined to turn from me.
Even though they call me God Most High,
I will by no means exalt them.

How can I give you up, Ephraim?
How can I hand you over, Israel?
How can I treat you like Admah?
How can I make you like Zeboyim?
My heart is changed within me;
all my compassion is aroused.
I will not carry out my fierce anger,
nor will I devastate Ephraim again.
For I am God, and not a man—
the Holy One among you.
I will not come against their cities.

Hosea 11:7–9 (NIV)

The people of Israel constantly disobeyed God, but God's love never failed them. He still had the plan to sacrifice Jesus for their sins and ours.

It was the goodness of God that transformed my heart to be sold out to Jesus. I pray that you, too, will encounter first love in Jesus and be left transformed.

Take time to read the Bible, and ask God to open your eyes and overwhelm you with the revelation of His love. That may be the season when you will experience first love for the first time.

Falling in Love with God

We all desire to fall in love, but the perception is that we can only experience it when we are in a relationship. The truth is that as a single person, you can experience the feeling of falling in love with God.

When I broke up with my boyfriend, the first couple of months were hard. Every time I saw a happy couple together, I thought to myself, *I'm missing out*. I missed the feeling of falling in love.

My boyfriend was always the first person on my mind when I woke up and the last person on my mind when I was about to go to sleep. I always looked forward to reading his texts. He was someone I could go to when I was discouraged.

So when God told me to let go of the relationship, I felt empty. For a while, I thought single life was supposed to be empty until I could again find someone to be in a relationship with. But through my season of singleness, God opened my eyes to see that I didn't need anyone to experience falling in love. God showed me that I could fall in love *with Him*.

I learned to turn to God when things were tough and I had no one else to turn to. I went deeper into His presence and His Word. His words and promises were what I held on to morning and night. I started putting sticky notes of God's promises on the walls of my room to remind myself of His love and faithfulness when everything seemed hopeless.

God became my first thought every morning and the last voice I heard every night. He became my comfort and love when I had no one else to draw from.

As I continued to seek God in my alone times, He revealed Himself and led me to scriptures or devotionals I needed. Jesus said in John 6:35 (NIV), "I am the bread of life. Whoever comes to me will never go hungry, and whoever believes in me will never be thirsty."

I found God to be the daily bread I needed every day. The more He revealed Himself to me, the more I fell in love with Him. Sometimes the only way to see God as our everything is to have only Him as our everything.

I was definitely in a season where God stripped many things from my life. I soon saw that He did this only so I would truly see His beauty and goodness.

Prior to asking me to let go of my second boyfriend, God asked me to let go of two other things that were very dear to my heart. First, He asked me to let go of my piano studio.

Letting Go of My Piano Studio

During college, I had invested four years into establishing my music studio. I had 26 piano students and held yearly recitals. I grew very attached to my students. When I graduated from college and started working full-time, it became obvious that I couldn't handle teaching 26 students, working full-time, and managing Living Revelations. I prayed and felt God nudging me to let go of my music studio.

I disobeyed God, however, and held on to my music studio by hiring an assistant teacher to teach my students. The teacher I hired ended up trying to steal my students. My students told me this was going on, so I stopped using the assistant teacher.

The incident opened my eyes to the reality that God truly meant it when He told me I needed to let my music studio go. It was hard, but I eventually let go of my students and told them about the new season God was opening up for me.

Sometimes God will ask us to let go of some good things because they aren't the *best things* for us. I ended up so thankful that I let go of my music studio because I was able to focus on Living Revelations and the ministries God was opening up for me.

I thought that was the end of having to let go of things dear to me, but little did I know that God wasn't done working in my heart.

Letting Go of Pursuing My Master's Degree

Six months after letting go of my music studio, I had plans to start taking courses toward my master's degree in business. The University of Florida had an amazing one-year program for students who already had a bachelor's degree in business. The university also had a perfect schedule for people who were working full-time. It sounded like a perfect plan; however, *God had different plans.* During my alone time, God told me to let it go.

I told God, *But everyone I know has a master's degree! I've been planning to pursue this for years.* Then I happened to listen to a podcast that was very timely. It talked about how our identity as a child of God should be enough—not our success, degrees, or accomplishments.

I realized that I had put a lot of my identity in my education and my accomplishments. It was hard for me to let go of pursuing my master's degree because I had put my identity in that degree. God then reminded me how He has always been faithful and to trust Him that letting this go would be best for me.

Looking back, I am thankful I didn't spend $45,000 on a master's degree. At the time, my goal was to work my way up the corporate ladder, but God called me to a path of full-time ministry and growing Living Revelations. Having the master's degree would have put me in debt.

Because I did not pursue my master's degree, I was also able to give myself to Bible classes at my church. That helped me pursue my call to disciple others in our online Bible studies. Once again, God knew what was best for me.

Sometimes we have to look back at our lives in order to understand God's ways. His plans may seem crazy, but later we realize that His plans were always perfect. We have choices in our lives, but may our desire be to choose God's perfect will and not settle for anything less.

Letting Go of My Boyfriend

After letting go of my music studio and a master's degree, God then asked me to let go of my second boyfriend. It was the hardest thing I've had to do. Singleness was my greatest fear, and God definitely knew that. Although I had fears in my heart, deep inside I knew God was faithful. I was already developing a track record with Him and could look back and see that He had always been faithful in what He had asked me to give up.

Unfortunately, I delayed my obedience and didn't break up with my boyfriend for two years. In the midst of those two years, God would never stop convicting me of my disobedience.

God used my parents and close friends to speak to my life. My close friend, who was also my mentor, invited me to have lunch and spoke to me heart-to-heart. She shared how she felt my relationship was suffocating my own relationship with God. She shared that God has someone for me who will take me where I need to be.

I was so shocked that she knew my exact feelings. I didn't have to explain the details of the complications of this relationship.

I knew I wasn't happy, and my relationship with God was suffocating by being with my second boyfriend. I was falling into impurity, and he was pulling me away from the ministry opportunities God had opened up for me.

During those two years, my parents also questioned if I was feeling true joy with my boyfriend. My mom then spoke prophetically to me and said I was putting my relationship over Jesus.

My stubborn heart wanted to deny the truth, but the conviction from the Lord never left me. Deep inside, I knew I was putting my relationship above Jesus. I knew I could never say Jesus was my everything if I wasn't willing to obey all He had asked of me. I was telling God that He could have everything in my life except my relationship.

The reality hit me that I couldn't live this way anymore. I realized that if I wanted to profess myself as a follower and lover of Jesus, I had to give Him my all.

Jesus said it Himself. "Whoever wants to be my disciple must deny themselves and take up their cross and follow me" (Matthew 16:24 NIV). I knew I could only experience His full blessings if I obeyed Him fully.

Then I was led to read 1 Samuel 15 and became convicted that I was trying to give God sacrifices over obedience. God clearly says He longs for our obedience rather than our sacrifice.

God told King Saul to attack the Amalekites and destroy everything that belonged to them. But King Saul disobeyed God and did not destroy everything.

> But Saul and the army spared Agag and the best of the sheep and cattle, the fat calves and lambs—everything that was good. These they were unwilling to destroy completely, but everything that was despised and weak they totally destroyed.
>
> 1 Samuel 15:9 (NIV)

King Saul then gave Samuel the prophet the excuse that he kept the fattened lamb to make sacrifices to God. Samuel responded on God's behalf. "Does the LORD delight in burnt offerings and sacrifices as much as in obeying the LORD? To obey is better than sacrifice" (1 Samuel 15:22 NIV).

When I read this passage, the Holy Spirit convicted me that I had been offering God my sacrifices but not my obedience. I was telling God that I would serve Him while still with my boyfriend and that I would convince my boyfriend to serve God alongside me. But my sacrifice was not what God was looking for. He was looking for my obedience.

Finally, after two years, I learned I could not live the fulfilled life if I didn't live to do the will of God. I broke up with my boyfriend and started my amazing journey in the Lord.

Growing Our Faith

As I look back, I can clearly see that God knew I was at the level to step out in greater faith and break up with my boyfriend. God asked me to let go of certain things in stages, not everything all at once. He knew I would come out stronger through each test.

You are capable of doing whatever God is asking of you. He is faithful to strengthen you and would never ask you to do something you are not able to do. Philippians 4:13 reminds us that we can do all things through Christ who strengthens us.

Our faith process with God will never end. Our tests will be harder each time but only so our faith can grow.

Abraham was someone who grew strong in his faith. "Yet he did not waver through unbelief regarding the promise of God, but was strengthened in his faith and gave glory to God" (Romans 4:20 NIV).

God was growing my faith so I could *trust Him more.* No matter where we are in life, there is always more room to trust God. There may be good things in life, but not all good things are best for us.

I believe God wants to develop a track record with you in this season. It may seem painful, but *trust His process.* Your obedience to God will cause you to fall in love with Him because it's only through obedience that you will see God's faithfulness come through.

If you're not willing to follow God's recipe, you can't blame Him when the outcome of your choices end up hurting you. But if you are willing to obey God and keep His ways, you can be sure to experience His goodness.

I am now married to my amazing husband, which could not have happened if I hadn't broken up with my previous boyfriend. God gave me a husband who has the same passion and desire that I have to build God's kingdom here on earth.

My last boyfriend may have been good, but he wasn't the best for me. God had a purpose for me. Like my mentor always told me, "You need someone who will take you where you need to be."

My husband, Michael, has been an immense support in God's calling in my life. We are able to work together to establish God's purposes here on earth. I honestly cannot imagine doing life with anyone but Michael, which is all for the glory of God.

God, too, has someone special for you—someone who will take you where you need to be and grow the very passions God has placed in your heart. Remember, *it's never worth settling for less than God's best.*

Jesus Is Enough

Throughout my life's journey, I have learned that there is nothing that can satisfy us more than Jesus. Fame, success, marriage, and everything else are never truly enough.

Only Jesus Satisfies

I've tried chasing after relationships to fill the void in me. While I would experience temporary satisfaction, I would be left feeling emptier. I now realize that when Jesus isn't a priority in our lives, we leave a void in our hearts that nothing but Jesus can fill.

We see this with the Samaritan woman in the Bible. In John 4, we see a woman who had five husbands and was currently with a man who wasn't her husband. Jesus told the woman that whoever drinks the water He gives will never thirst (John 4:14). Jesus wasn't talking about our physical hunger; He was referring to our *spiritual hunger.* He wanted the woman to know that only *He could satisfy her soul.* Only He could leave her *thirsty for no more.*

I believe the Samaritan woman knew that deep inside she was empty and was longing for something more. She desired satisfaction, but nothing in the world, even her relationships, could fill that void. Jesus revealed to her that He was the Messiah, the one they all had been waiting for to save them.

That was the day the woman realized that all she needed was the man sitting in front of her. *She received her wake-up call.*

What about you? Have you received your wake-up call that *only Jesus satisfies?*

If Jesus is our true satisfaction, why have we put other things above Him? Why is it hard for us to let go of relationships when we know that our relationship with Jesus is the only one that satisfies?

We have to remember that as humans, we have a body, soul, and spirit. The reason that success, fame, and people can never satisfy is because they were never meant to satisfy our spirit and our soul.

Jesus was made to satisfy our soul. As long as we keep pursuing other things, we will always be left feeling empty and wanting more. Psalm 23:3 (NASB) says, "He restores my soul."

Jesus is the only one who will complete our joy. He must be our primary pursuit, and as we seek Him, everything else will be given to us (Matthew 6:33).

Draw Close to God

Make it your prayer every day to ask God to reveal Himself to you. God has given you the Holy Spirit to lead you into all truth and speak to you what you need. I always make this verse my prayer before getting into my alone times with Jesus.

> But when he, the Spirit of truth, comes, he will guide you into all the truth. He will not speak on his own; he will speak only what he hears, and he will tell you what is yet to come.
>
> John 16:13 (NIV)

Many times we compartmentalize our times to hear from God. We may only open the door for God to speak to us twice a day—morning and night. The truth is that God wants to speak to us throughout the day. Instead of closing God off for the whole day, we should be opening our ears to hear from Him anytime and anywhere. The more we spend time with God, the more we will *fall in love with Him.*

Our times with Jesus don't always have to be in our room and on our knees. Yes, we must meet Jesus in the secret place and have that quality time with Him, but that shouldn't be the only time. "But Jesus often withdrew to lonely places and prayed" (Luke 5:16 NIV).

Think about how you would treat your loved ones. I'm sure you're not talking to them only once a day. You text them and talk to them whenever you get the chance, whether it's in the middle of work or school and afterwards. God wants us to talk and listen to Him *whenever and wherever we are.*

The more we hear from God, the more we will grow closer to Him and find Him real in our everyday lives. Paul tells us to "pray without ceasing" (1 Thessalonians 5:17 NASB). Take time to reserve moments throughout the day to take a quick five-minute break to pray to God. As you spend more time with God, your love for Him will grow.

Where are opportunities for you to talk and hear from God more? Maybe it's during your car rides home or during bathroom breaks. What about a lunch break with God?

I used to set lunch dates on certain days of the week just to spend time with God. He would reveal things to me that were very timely to hear.

God desires for us to sit before Him and listen to Him. As much as He loves us doing things for Him, He values our ears and eyes on Him.

In Luke we read about Mary and Martha. "She had a sister called Mary, who sat at the Lord's feet listening to what he said. But Martha was distracted by all the preparations that had to be made" (Luke 10:39–40 NIV).

Jesus said to Martha, "Mary has chosen what is better" (Luke 10:42 NIV).

Are we spending more of our time *doing things for God or listening to Him?* If we want to draw closer to God, it's not by doing more for Him or going to more conferences and church services. It is simply by giving our attention and time to Jesus.

We need to read our Bible every day because God speaks to us through His Word. "In the beginning was the Word, and the Word was with God, and the Word was God" (John 1:1 NIV).

God is the Word, so in the Bible, we will be able to know Him more. Many times we find ourselves listening to what others say about God—watching preachers or speakers on TV—but we neglect the Word of God itself.

Imagine dating someone, and the things you know about them are only what other people say about them. It's obvious that the result of this is lack of time and intimacy with the person. Jesus wants you to know Him *personally.*

Paul writes in Hebrews 5 that we ought to reach a point where we can eat solid food and not be fed milk by others. As we spend time in His Word, the Holy Spirit will give us direct revelations of who Jesus is.

Drawing closer to Jesus starts with spending time with Jesus.

Just like dating is required in any relationship, we have to set time to date God. Dating is spending quality time with someone.

Jesus longs to draw you into His arms and refresh you with His waterfalls of love and revelation. David wrote, "Deep calls to deep in the roar of your waterfalls; all your waves and breakers have swept over me" (Psalm 42:7 NIV). We can go deep and see the depths of Jesus's heart if we give Him our undivided attention and obedience. It's in the depths of His heart that we find ourselves falling more in love with the person of Jesus.

Jesus always sends you an invitation to come and follow Him. He asked His disciples to follow Him. It's up to you to let go of everything and follow Him. "Draw near to God, and he will draw near to you. Cleanse your hands, you sinners, and purify your hearts, you double-minded" (James 4:8 ESV).

Getting closer to God starts with our willingness to follow Him no matter where He asks us to go.

God's love is better than any other love story you could ever have. There is no love that surpasses God's love. No one can love you more than God.

You must have a relationship with God if you want to experience His love. Christianity was never about religious acts; it was about falling in love with Jesus. We were never created to come to God with dread; God wanted us to come to Him joyfully. "Your love, LORD, reaches to the heavens, your faithfulness to the skies" (Psalm 36:5 NIV).

God loved us so much that He sent His only Son, Jesus, to die for our sins. Jesus died and rose again so we can have life abundantly now and forever. God wants us to experience His love now on earth.

Are you falling in love with God? Are you excited to spend time with God, or is time with God the last thing on your to-do list?

Our Father in heaven wants to have a relationship with you. *Will you accept God's love and do life with Him?*

God loves you so much and wants you to fall in love with Him. You don't need to search for love elsewhere because God's love is available now for you.

You will find yourself falling in love like never before when you take the time to build a relationship with God. He has the ability to surprise you, encourage you, and love you like no other.

Hidden in Christ

Perhaps you have heard this saying: You need to be made whole before getting into a relationship. That statement is valid, but no matter how whole you are, there are greater levels of intimacy with Christ that you can experience when you are *hidden in Him*.

We are all called to be hidden in Christ in all seasons of our lives (Colossians 3:3), but there is a uniqueness that comes when we are hidden in Christ as a single person. Paul even said that as married people, our hearts are divided.

> I would like you to be free from concern. An unmarried man is concerned about the Lord's affairs—how he can please the Lord. But a married man is concerned about the affairs of this world—how he can please his wife—and his interests are divided. An unmarried woman or virgin is concerned about the Lord's affairs: Her aim is to be devoted to the Lord in both body and spirit. But a married woman is concerned about the affairs of this world—how she can please her husband.
>
> 1 Corinthians 7:32–34 (NIV)

You have the opportunity in your single season to give your undivided attention to Jesus. It is the time for Him to transform you into a beautiful butterfly and for you to thrive in your God-given purpose.

I have already mentioned how God used the cocoon and butterfly phases to speak to me during my single season. There came a point when I believed I met the one—Michael—who is now my husband. However, I remember God telling me I was still in my cocoon phase and to stay there. There were still things in me that God wanted to work through, and they could only be done if I stayed single.

Before a caterpillar can turn into a butterfly, it must go through its cocoon stage. The caterpillar stays in the chrysalis alone and develops into a butterfly. Inside the cocoon, the caterpillar is transforming into a new creature. Its old body dies, and its new body develops. When we accept Jesus as our Savior and walk in Him, our old life dies, and we become new creations. "Therefore, if anyone is in Christ, the new creation has come: The old has gone, the new is here!" (2 Corinthians 5:17 NIV).

Our journey of growth doesn't end when we accept Jesus. There is a sanctifying process that happens in us as we hide ourselves in Christ. It's during our single season that we have the opportunity to grow stronger in our relationship with the Lord.

During our single season when we're hidden in Christ, it can seem like nothing is happening. However, there is a lot of transformation happening inside of us that we can't see at the moment. When you look at a cocoon from the outside, it looks as if nothing is happening. But if you wait for a certain time to pass, you will see that the caterpillar inside the cocoon is now a butterfly.

We can become that butterfly if we choose to stay hidden in Christ and allow Him to do the work He longs to do in our lives. If the caterpillar is taken out of its cocoon phase too early, its butterfly wings will break. This same concept applies to us. If we leave our single season too soon, we may break and falter because God hasn't finished the work He wanted to do in us as single people.

God may want to strengthen your relationship with Him during this season so you don't need to rely on a partner. The hardest thing about a breakup is going through life feeling alone. It can almost seem impossible to go through life single; however, we need to trust that with God, all things are possible. God wants to show you in this season that *He is enough*.

Maybe you are struggling with knowing your identity in Christ. He wants to solidify that in you so your identity and value aren't tied to someone else or what someone else thinks.

Whatever transformation God wants to do in you during your single season, trust the process.

This is not to say that we are perfect people once we get married. God is constantly perfecting us through every season of life. We are to always go from *glory to glory* (2 Corinthians 3:18).

For the longest time, I dreaded even the thought of needing to be single. I told God I could still serve Him even if I was with someone. But God wasn't concerned with how much I could do for Him. He was concerned with how much I would *trust Him*. It's easy for us to say that we can live life as a single person, but if the time comes when God asks you to let go of a relationship, will you?

If there is even a slight hesitancy to let go of anything for Christ in your life, that means you don't completely trust God. It shows God there is more work to be done in your heart in order to rely on Him. It also shows that God is not first priority in your life.

I tried convincing God every day that I didn't need to go through my cocoon phase, but He knew better. God also knows what you need and what process you have to go through to solidify your faith in Him.

> Consider it pure joy, my brothers and sisters, whenever you face trials of many kinds, because you know that the testing of your faith produces perseverance. Let perseverance finish its work so that you may be mature and complete, not lacking anything.
>
> James 1:2–4 (NIV)

I tried very hard to convince God to allow me to stay in my relationship before Michael. I made deals with God and told Him I'd pray every day for Him to change and that we could grow in the Word together.

I even tried to convince myself that being with my boyfriend was the right thing to do. I had dated him for three years, and our families got along well together. Looking back, I realize that when we are desperate for something, we can make any excuse to justify our actions. In the end, I couldn't shake off the conviction that I knew God wanted me to let go of that relationship.

God always reminded me of James 1:2–4, and I knew deep inside that I would never be ready to fulfill my God-given purpose if I didn't pass this test of letting go of my boyfriend. James makes it clear that we must persevere through trials so we can be mature, complete, and lacking nothing.

If we find ourselves trying to convince God to let us have our way, we must stop and reflect on our own motives. *Are we trying to convince God because we don't trust in His ways?*

It can be tempting to give in to our flesh and stay in relationships that God says no to. It's during those moments that we must remember God's purpose for our lives—that it's not worth being with someone when God knows that person will pull us away from Him.

We must remember that God is a *good God*. If He's asking us to let go of someone, that means He has a better spouse for us. It means He has a spouse who fits into the purpose God created us for—someone we can enjoy life with.

The biggest lie I held on to for so long was that I wouldn't meet someone I would love and that God would approve of. I was obviously wrong because I met Michael, who has been an amazing husband and partner as we pursue God's assignments.

During my season of singleness, there was one lady who always spoke into my life. She told me, "Before you can help others, you must first be qualified to help them."

That made sense. Before you can be a doctor, you must first pass a series of tests and prove you can help others.

I knew deep inside that God wanted me to help other singles get in the right relationships and walk in purity, but there was no way I could do that if I continued to stay in the relationship before Michael. Praise God that I obeyed Him, and here I am writing this book to help you walk through your single season.

I didn't want to live my life thinking, *What if I had obeyed God? What would my life have looked like?* When we obey God, we can be assured that we will see His faithfulness in our lives. We don't have to fear failure or disappointment because God is never a God who disappoints. He always gives us exceedingly and abundantly above all we could ever ask or imagine (Ephesians 3:20).

Maybe you're thinking, *I can still grow with God while being in a relationship.* That is true. During the time I dated Michael, both of our relationships with God grew deeper and stronger. But that only happened because we both dated in God's right timing. It happened because I allowed God to do the work He longed to do in me during my cocoon phase. I was ready to be in a relationship.

Prior to my single season, relationships always pulled me away from God. I always prioritized my boyfriend over God. But after going through my cocoon phase, God became my true foundation. I no longer had to fear that Michael would pull me away from God. We were able to grow in God together because we were both rooted in Him and not each other.

If God has been calling you to be single, trust that there is a transformation for you during this time. You may be whole, but there is more depth and intimacy.

> I remain confident of this:
>> I will see the goodness of the LORD
>> in the land of the living.
> Wait for the LORD;
>> be strong and take heart
>> and wait for the LORD.
>> Psalm 27:13–14 (NIV)

Don't rush into a relationship. God knows the best person and the right timing. Be strong and wait for God. When you allow Jesus to be the Shepherd of your life, you can be sure you will see His faithfulness come to pass.

Ask God in this season to take you deeper into His heart. If you aren't sure if you are in a season to date, ask God. He will show you as you spend time in His Word and allow the Holy Spirit to lead you into truth.

You're Not Alone

What is the first thing that comes to your mind when you think of being single? For me, it was being alone. For the longest time, the thought of being single scared me.

I thought, *I have no one to fall back on when things get bad, no one to help me when I need help, and no one to comfort me in my hardest moments.* It was in that moment that God told me, "You're not alone, and you were never alone. I am with you."

I've heard many people tell me, "Don't worry. God is with you." It never clicked with me until God's words rang in my heart.

I realized then that the God who split the Red Sea and made a way for the Israelites was with me. The God who led Gideon and 300 men to defeat a whole army of Midianites was with me. The God who helped David defeat the unbeatable Goliath was with me. The God who gave his beloved Son, Jesus, to save us was with me.

The same God who did the impossible back then is the same God who wants to do the impossible with *your life today.* You're not alone. You were never alone. God is with you. We don't have to be afraid of doing life alone because we have the most powerful and mighty God with us at all times.

When I look back at my life, I realize that God was always with me through the good and the bad. Even when

I was far from God and living in disobedience, He never stopped pursuing me.

Sometimes we can easily forget how much God loves us. When we do bad things, we question if He's with us. But the reality is that He is always with us and longs for us to welcome Him into our hearts. "But God shows his love for us in that while we were still sinners, Christ died for us" (Romans 5:8 ESV). If God loved us while we were sinners, why do we question His love for us now?

God loves us, and it's the revelation of His love that will cause our hearts to turn to Him and away from our sinful life. Though there may be times you will fall, know that Jesus is right by your side, willing to pick you back up and do life with you. Jesus is not looking for perfect lives; He is looking for *hearts that are pursuing God*.

David in the Bible was a man who made many mistakes, but God still called Him a man after His own heart. *Why?* Because despite his faults, David repented, turned away from his sins, and gave his heart to God. His desire was to honor and love the Lord. Though his journey wasn't perfect, his heart was set on the Lord.

David knew he could always cry out to God despite his faults. We, too, must acknowledge that we are not alone. God hears our cries. He's seen our wrongdoings and yet still loves us. We can come to God with confidence because of what Jesus did for us on the cross.

He is calling on our hearts to come into fellowship with Him.

David wrote, "Have mercy on me, O God, according to your unfailing love; according to your great compassion blot out my transgressions" (Psalm 51:1 NIV).

When we come to Jesus and confess our sins with a changed heart, He purifies us from all unrighteousness. "If we confess our sins, he is faithful and just and will forgive us our sins and purify us from all unrighteousness" (1 John 1:9 NIV).

Whatever you have done, you can still come to Jesus and know that He will forgive you. Ask Him to change your heart, and then commit every day to seeking Him and renewing your mind with His truth.

You're not alone just because you are single. You have a God who is with you and for you.

Do Not Fear

> So do not fear, for I am with you;
> do not be dismayed, for I am your God.
> I will strengthen you and help you;
> I will uphold you with my righteous
> right hand.
>
> Isaiah 41:10 (NIV)

We don't need to be afraid of doing life alone because we're not alone. We have a mighty God who is with us and for us. God is here to help us because He wants the best for us.

In the book of Judges in the Bible, we see God telling Gideon to take his men and defeat the Midianites, who were very powerful at the time. Gideon's army was weak. Here's how Gideon responded to God. "Pardon me, my lord...but how can I save Israel? My clan is the weakest in Manasseh, and I am the least in my family" (Judges 6:15 NIV).

God responded to Gideon, "I will be with you, and you will strike down all the Midianites, leaving none alive" (Judges 6:16 NIV).

God didn't need Gideon to have a strong army because God was strong enough to defeat the Midianites. In fact, God told Gideon to strip down his army to only 300 men to fight against the thousands of Midianites.

Why did God ask Gideon to only bring 300 men? Because God wanted Gideon to know that *He was enough*. God wants you to know that *He is enough*.

He is enough to get you through your single season. He is enough to get you through school. He is enough to provide for you and for the rest of your needs. God *knows* your needs (Matthew 6:8).

Of course, two people are always better than one, but if God is calling you to be single in this season, know that you have everything you need. You don't need someone besides God to get where you need to be. He may want to teach you in this season to see Him as your everything.

God must become the foundation we stand on. When Jesus is our rock, nothing can shake us.

> Therefore everyone who hears these words of mine and puts them into practice is like a wise man who built his house on the rock. The rain came down, the streams rose, and the winds blew and beat against that house; yet it did not fall, because it had its foundation on the rock. But everyone who hears these words of mine and does not put them into practice is like a foolish man who built his house on sand.
>
> Matthew 7:24–26 (NIV)

What is God saying to you in this season? Have you been obeying what He is putting in your heart to do? God only tells us to do things so we can see Him come through for us. Just as He came through for Gideon, He wants to come through for you.

Maybe you're feeling like I was—weak and alone. Remember, you can be *strong* when you go through your single season. "I can do all things through Christ who strengthens me" (Philippians 4:13 NKJV).

Kris Swiatocho, director of the Singles Network, once said, "You may feel lonely, but you're not alone." We must not let our emotions of loneliness make us settle for less than God's best. Don't be afraid to ask God for strength through your single season. There will be moments when you will feel weak and lonely. Use those moments to run back to Jesus.

Open Up to God

We don't have to be afraid to open up to God. Many of us struggle to open up because of fear that others will look down on us. People may use our weaknesses against us, but God never will. We can open up to God and trust that He will transform our hearts.

God never asked us to do things in our own strength but in His strength. He never expected us to go through life without needing His help and comfort. God wants us to come to Him with our brokenness. "Trust in him at all times, you people; pour out your hearts to him, for God is our refuge" (Psalm 62:8 NIV).

God wants to be your place of refuge. A refuge is a place of shelter and comfort from trouble. God wants to be the place where you find comfort from the troubles and worries this world may bring. There's no better place to find healing and peace than going to God.

We may think that forgetting our pain and anxiety will do us no harm, but it actually will. Suppressing our pain is like taking painkillers when we should be taking medicine that will heal us. Painkillers temporarily numb the pain, but they will never completely heal the pain. The pain will come back in a matter of time.

When we suppress our emotions, things only get worse in time. Hiding our pain will not heal us, but bringing it to Jesus will. Bring your worries to Jesus, and He will heal you and fill you with His peace.

> Do not be anxious about anything, but in every situation, by prayer and petition, with thanksgiving, present your requests to God. And the peace of God, which transcends all understanding, will guard your hearts and your minds in Christ Jesus.
>
> Philippians 4:6–7 (NIV)

Will you open up your heart to God and allow Him to speak life over you? God can't fix what you don't give Him. He can only heal those who are willing to come to Him with their brokenness. Jesus once asked a blind man named Bartimaeus, "What do you want me to do for you?" Bartimaeus answered, "I want to see" (Mark 10:51 NIV).

Jesus is asking you right now, *What do you want?*

We can choose to either run away from our struggles or *bring them to Jesus.* Instead of justifying our weaknesses, we need to see them as they are and come before Jesus, asking Him to heal our broken hearts. Confess your struggles and weaknesses to God because it's only then that He can transform you and strengthen you.

Connect with a Community

During your single season, be sure to stay close and connected to a community of people who love God and are walking in His truth. If you don't have a community of believers to connect to, pray and ask God to bring you one.

During my single season, I felt God leading me to the singles ministry at my church. I happened to see a video of the singles pastor sharing a message on Facebook, and it really spoke to me. I decided to attend the group's weekly prayer meetings, which ended up helping me through my single season.

There were moments when I was tempted to go back to my ex-boyfriend, but whenever I attended those prayer meetings, various people spoke timely words of encouragement to me—simple words like "don't settle for less than God's best" or "don't back-slide but front-slide to Jesus." They reminded me to continue running the course.

I left those prayer meetings feeling refreshed and fueled to continue to persevere. We must remember that we're not created to live life alone. The enemy will try to isolate us so we will give in to his lies and discouragement, but God has given us community to speak life into us. "Therefore encourage one another and build each other up" (1 Thessalonians 5:11 NIV).

I didn't join the singles ministry to find a spouse, but I did end up meeting my husband there. You never know how God will lead you as you faithfully seek Him.

Confess Your Struggles to Someone

Not only is getting connected to a community important, but also confessing your struggles and sins to others who are walking with the Lord.

Therefore confess your sins to each other and pray for each other so that you may be healed. The prayer of a righteous person is powerful and effective.

James 5:16 (NIV)

Your healing will come as you confess your sins and pray with someone.

I was still struggling with the fear of singleness even after obeying God and walking through my single season. I couldn't shake it off. I ended up going to a women's conference, and during the altar call, I felt the Lord calling me to go up.

I really didn't want to go, but God's nudge was very strong. As I walked toward the altar, I had already planned to just stand there and not ask anyone for prayer. I didn't feel like confessing my fears to someone, but God knew I needed to.

The moment I got to the altar, a familiar voice started calling my name.

"Gaby! Gaby!"

I looked up to see the lady who had taught my Bible classes at my church. I thank God that she was determined to pray for me because I didn't realize how much I needed it.

As she gripped my hands, she asked me how she could pray for me, and it was then that I confessed to her my fear of singleness. We both prayed together that the fear would break, and she also started praying for my future husband.

After praying with her that day, I experienced a great breakthrough. I felt the stronghold of the fear of singleness break off of me. As we both declared my future spouse in God's hand, confidence started arising within my heart.

There is power when we confess our struggles and pray with someone. If you have been struggling over fears, anxiety, lust, or other things, confess it with someone you know who has a holy fear of the Lord. Their prayers are powerful and will help bring about your breakthrough.

It's okay to have weaknesses because it's then that we can see God's strength displayed. "My grace is sufficient for you, for my power is made perfect in weakness" (2 Corinthians 12:9 NIV).

Jesus Is Your Missing Piece

This is the season where God wants to show you that He is the missing piece in your life. It can be easy to think that we are missing something when we don't have a boy-friend or husband, but the reality is that Jesus is all we need.

For the longest time, I thought that having a husband would complete me. God showed me that only He can complete me. I kept feeling like I was missing something because I was filling my heart with the wrong thing.

Jesus is the missing piece to complete us. "The LORD is my portion; therefore I will wait for him" (Lamentations 3:24 NIV). This verse reminds us that God—not a successful career, not a spouse, not a family—is our portion. He is our missing piece to complete our soul.

What have you been trying to fill your emptiness with? Will you seek God and make Him your portion?

We can rest knowing that when we put our hope in God, He will never fail us. He is good and will leave us filled—never empty. "The LORD is good to those whose hope is in him, to the one who seeks him" (Lamentations 3:25 NIV).

It can be easy to turn to friends or relationships when things are tough. That's great, but we must remember that Jesus is the true remedy for our soul. Invite the Holy Spirit to speak to you and lead you into the truth that you need to hear each and every day.

Look to God to fill your empty soul. He desires to fill the desires of your heart, but He first wants you to learn to delight in Him. "Delight yourself in the LORD, and he will give you the desires of your heart" (Psalm 37:4 ESV). We must understand that God is what we need, and everything else is desires. Once we believe this truth, God will allow all our other desires to fall into place.

Will you surrender your life to a mighty God and trust that your life is in good hands? Will you step out in faith and do what God has called you to do, knowing that He goes with you?

It can be tempting to take things into your own hands and get into relationships you know are not of God. But remember to *not settle for less than God's best.*

May we be like the woman described in Proverbs 31:25 (NLT): "She is clothed with strength and dignity, and she laughs without fear of the future."

You can live life boldly because God is with you and for you. You're not alone.

Lord, I thank you that I don't need to live in fear because You are always with me, and I am never alone. I thank You that I can thrive in my single season knowing that You are for me.

Let's Be Real

Often we suppress the truth with excuses to get what we want. What if the truth we have been pushing off for so long is truly what we need to hear? It's time to be real with ourselves.

For the longest time, I tried ignoring the truth that my ex-boyfriend didn't fit into the call God had for my life. I loved serving God in my college ministry, but my boyfriend didn't. I was falling in love with the Word of God, but he was falling away from the Word. I wanted purity, but he wanted sex. He had no appreciation for what I was called to do and questioned it instead.

I came up with many excuses to run away from the truth until I finally had no more reasons. I had to face the fact that I would either *walk with God or walk away from God*. Choosing to stay with my ex-boyfriend was choosing to walk away from God. I had to be real with myself and understand that this relationship wasn't God's will.

Many times, we try to convince ourselves that we are walking with God when we clearly know that the one we are dating is only pulling us away from God. Instead of making excuses and claiming to be a Christian who walks with Jesus, it is better that we confess what we're doing.

When we confess that we are disobeying God, the Holy Spirit can then bring us conviction that will lead us to walk in the way of truth. It may take a while, but conviction will bring us to repentance and truth.

I had to accept that if I stayed in this relationship, God would choose someone else to complete the purpose He had for my life. Was I ready to live life knowing that this would happen?

No, I wasn't, which is why, in the end, I broke up with my boyfriend. I didn't want to live life thinking, *What if I had obeyed God? What would my life have been like?* My walk of obedience with God started from *being real with myself and God.*

If you've been running away from the truth, now is the time to confess it and *own up to it.* The only way to be healed and transformed is to confess your sins to Jesus and change. You may feel weak and unable to do the right thing, but the grace of God will strengthen you.

> If we claim to be without sin, we deceive ourselves and the truth is not in us. If we confess our sins, he is faithful and just and will forgive us our sins and purify us from all unrighteousness.
>
> 1 John 1:8–9 (NIV)

The truth of God is what will set us free (John 8:32).

What truths have you laid hidden away from your life? This is the season to pick back up the convictions the Holy Spirit laid upon your heart. Conviction is meant to draw us back to the will of God. We must have the heart that only wants God's will because only His will is good for us.

> Do not conform to the pattern of this world, but be transformed by the renewing of your

mind. Then you will be able to test and
approve what God's will is—his good, pleasing and perfect will.

Romans 12:2 (NIV)

We must renew our minds with God's truth. Instead of
entertaining our own fears or desires, let's entertain the truth
that God is always faithful and always has the best in store
for us.

Your faith in Jesus means nothing if you don't do something with it. Allow your faith to move you in *complete surrender* to God. Not until you surrender your life to God will
you see His hand move on your life.

"You see that a person is justified by works and not by
faith alone" (James 2:24 ESV). Put your faith in action, and
discover how God can meet each of your desires. It's not
about what you know but *what you do with what you know.*

God wants you to experience a love and joy that will
fulfill you—as a single person now and in your future
relationship.

My Journey of Letting Go of My Boyfriend

I knew deep inside that my boyfriend wasn't the one.
We weren't walking the same path. I felt called to full-time
ministry, and he despised ministry life.

I was holding on to him only because I was afraid I
wouldn't find someone more fitting for me. *I was willing to
compromise God's best out of fear.*

But what I failed to do was filter my fears through the
eyes of God. I finally realized that if God loves me, He would
want the best for me. God had never failed me and had never

asked me to let go of something without giving me something better. So why was I choosing not to believe that He would do the same when it came to my future spouse?

Often we are willing to accept less than God's best to alleviate a fear that isn't even valid. God knows our desires, so why are we afraid He won't give us our desires?

As much as you don't want to be alone and single, know that God also doesn't want you to be alone and single. He longs to fulfill your desires, especially marriage, because marriage is the best representation of His covenant with us.

The fact that we are scared that God doesn't know what we need and won't give us what we need is a *false fear*. If that thought has been replaying in your mind, now is the time to stop it and throw it away.

"Delight yourself in the Lord, and he will give you the desires of your heart" (Psalm 37:4 ESV). If we profess the Bible to be true, then *we need to start living like what the Bible says is true*. The enemy is good at planting fears in our minds, but we must replace every fear with God's promises and truth.

When I finally had the courage to let my boyfriend go, the first couple of months were some of the hardest months of my life. Fear kept taunting my mind.

What if I never find anyone better than him? What if I end up miserable? I asked myself. *Am I really ready to just let go of a three-year investment I made with someone?*

Some nights I would just lie in bed and replay the sweet memories we had made over those three years. I felt horrible afterward. Finally, I realized why I was in such a bad condition. *Fear was on replay.*

Just as music has the power to affect our emotions, so do our thoughts, which have the power to affect our emotions and our soul. That is why Paul reminds us, "Whatever is true, whatever is noble, whatever is right, whatever is pure, whatever is lovely, whatever is admirable—if anything is excellent or praiseworthy—think about such things" (Philippians 4:8 NIV).

When we choose to think about praiseworthy thoughts—things that are lovely and pure—we will find ourselves full of joy and peace. We can't change our circumstances, but we can choose to change our perspective.

If we let fear reign in our minds, we will be left with a fearful heart. If we choose to let God's truth reign in our minds, we will find our hearts strengthened and transformed into the image of God.

I needed to remind myself that God has never failed me, and He will never fail me. We need to replace every fearful thought with God's truth. We can choose to replay our fears or replay God's faithfulness in our minds.

God Has the Best in Store for You

God only has the best for us, and He won't give us anything less. Don't expect the worst to come from what God is asking you to do. Believe that the best will come from doing what God asks you to do.

God's plans for your life are good, pleasing, and perfect—will you believe that? Will you push pause and delete every negative thought that is consuming your mind?

The first place the enemy will attack us is in our minds. If the enemy has control of our minds, he knows he can hold us back from pursuing God's will. Don't let the enemy take the best God has for you. "We demolish arguments and every pretension that sets itself up against the knowledge of God, and we take captive every thought to make it obedient to Christ" (2 Corinthians 10:5 NIV).

We have the power to control our fears. It starts with allowing Christ to reign over our thoughts.

Replace every fearful thought with God's truth.

If you're feeling doubtful that God knows best, replace that thought with this verse: "'*For I know the plans I have for you,' declares the LORD, 'plans to prosper you and not to harm you, plans to give you hope and a future.*'" (Jeremiah 29:11 NIV).

If you're feeling hopeless about your circumstances and feel like giving up, replay this verse in your heart.

> So do not throw away your confidence; it will
> be richly rewarded. You need to persevere so
> that when you have done the will of God,
> you will receive what he has promised.
> Hebrews 10:35–36 (NIV)

We must be intentional with what we let our minds replay. Choose to believe that God is good and that His ways are best. Nothing can strengthen us better than the Word of God.

God's plans for your life are only to prosper you and give you a good future. If you have any thought that speaks against this, then throw that thought away. With Christ, you can overcome any fear.

We don't have to lie to ourselves and say we don't want to be in a relationship. I know so many people who go through a breakup and say they don't want to be in a relationship. The truth is, if they met the right person, I am sure they would love to be in a relationship.

Instead of lying to ourselves to make ourselves feel better, we must lean on God's promises as our comfort. We don't have to be afraid that God won't come through with His promises. He always comes through, and He always gives us exceedingly above all that we could ever ask or imagine (Ephesians 3:20).

God came through for me and sent me my husband, who fits perfectly into the calling that God has for my life. We will enjoy marriage more as we embrace singleness and wait for the right one from God. Our single season is meant to prepare us to make the most of our married life.

If God came through for me, *He will also come through for you.*

Lord, I want Your promises to reign in my mind. Help me to replace all my fears with Your loving truth—that You are always good.

Adventuring with God

The journey in following Jesus will lead us to great places we could never imagine. However, it will also lead us to experience hardships and struggles. Jesus tells us that we will face tribulation but that we do not have to worry because *He has overcome the world* (John 16:33). That means that if Jesus has overcome the world, through Him we can live as overcomers.

Throughout the Old Testament, the Israelites defeated enemies who were far greater than they were. Gideon was asked to fight thousands of Midianites with only 300 men. The Israelites were asked to walk around the walls of Jericho and watch its walls come down. "By faith the walls of Jericho fell" (Hebrews 11:30 NIV).

It is not by our own strength that walls in our lives come down. It is by the *power of God activated through our faith.*

A life of adventuring with God starts with walking by faith. We must be willing to take a step forward when God says so, even when we can't see the outcome. *Faith is believing without seeing.* We are called to walk by faith and not by sight (2 Corinthians 5:7).

Part of the adventure is seeing God do the impossible in our lives. We will see Him do things we *could never do* without Him. "In all these things we are more than conquerors through him who loved us" (Romans 8:37 NIV).

Through Christ, we are called to overcome, to defeat the impossible, and to win battles *greater* than ourselves. "But we have this treasure in earthen vessels, that the excellence of the power may be of God and not of us" (2 Corinthians 4:7 NKJV). We are weak vessels through whom God chooses to manifest His power. When we choose to abide in Him, His glory shines through us (Psalm 67:1).

Jesus tells us, "And I will do whatever you ask in my name, so that the Father may be glorified in the Son" (John 14:13 NIV).

There is a condition to this promise to those who obey God. Jesus adds, "If you love me, keep my commands. And I will ask the Father, and he will give you another advocate to help you and be with you forever" (John 14:15–16 NIV).

The advocate Jesus is referring to is the Holy Spirit, whose role is to live inside of us and guide us to live life to the fullest. This is the key to a life of adventure. The definition of adventure is to engage in hazardous and exciting activity, especially the exploration of unknown territory.

I think the word *adventure* best describes the life of one who walks with God. Yes, we will be required to step out of our comfort zone and move to unknown places, but we can always be sure that Jesus is with us wherever we go. He promises to never leave us or forsake us (Deuteronomy 31:6).

My First Year of Being Single

The year I chose to obey God and be single was the year I grew the most in the Lord. As I obeyed and surrendered my life fully to God, He started opening doors. He helped me with the resources I needed to start Living Revelations Ministries and brought people into my life who were willing to serve.

Opportunities came about for me to speak at conferences and gatherings, and I didn't have to ask. It was also the year God started using me through prophetic messages. He revealed to me things about others—whether it was past hurts they had experienced or dreams hidden in their hearts. I saw many people encouraged and in awe at the power of Jesus.

As I was working out at the gym, God showed me things about people. This is the common response I heard: "I've never experienced this before. God must be real."

I found myself being an encouragement and influence to my family, friends, coworkers, and strangers who God brought to my attention.

That year I became single was also when I connected with my husband. I never imagined myself getting married within a year, but it happened. We faced some struggles with my parents, but through the struggles, we saw God move mightily upon their hearts.

Our wedding was beautiful, and many of our family and close friends cried to see how God had reconciled my family with my husband. It was evident that God was in our relationship.

My adventure with God is not over. I don't have all the answers nor do I know what will happen in five, ten, or many years to come. What I do know is that God is faithful and that the coming years will be ever more glorious.

If we choose to abide in God, we will see our lives go from glory to glory (2 Corinthians 3:18). God has big plans for us. "'What no eye has seen, what no ear has heard, and what no human mind has conceived'—the things God has prepared for those who love him" (1 Corinthians 2:9 NIV).

Just like many verses in the Bible, this verse is also a conditional verse. We are promised to have a great life beyond what we can imagine, but it is only promised to those who *love God.* The best way to show God our love is to obey and abide in His ways. Our flesh will always try to get in the way of that, but we must remember that following God is always the *better way.*

God will ask us to do things that don't make sense, but we must trust that He sees the bigger picture. There's no need for faith if everything is seen and laid out. God desires our faith to grow, which can only come by stepping into places we never knew were possible. God will ask you to do things that seem impossible, but it is only to prove to you that He is the God of the impossible.

Will You Follow Jesus?

Jesus once asked Peter to cast out his fishnets even though Peter and the other men had been fishing all night and had caught nothing. Peter obeyed Jesus despite how he felt, and to his surprise, his nets were so overflowing with fish that they broke, and the boat started sinking (Luke 5:6–7).

In that moment, Peter saw the power of Jesus. He saw that Jesus was truly the one to be followed. Peter left all the fish and followed Jesus. Peter learned that *Jesus was worth* leaving everything for.

Will you leave everything behind and follow Jesus? Do you see Jesus worth leaving everything for?

Jesus's invitation to His disciples was "Come, follow me" (Matthew 4:19 NIV). The invitation to follow Jesus is to know Him more deeply and to see His glory manifested in your life.

We should not wait until we have no fear to step out and follow Jesus. It's our small step of obedience *today* that matters. Our willingness to surrender it all to Jesus *despite what we feel* is what will take us to a place where we will be in awe at the wonders of Jesus.

If Peter never took that step of obedience, he would have missed out on seeing the glorious power of Jesus and an amazing life of adventure with Him.

It's hard to follow Jesus and leave your comfort zone, but you can rest assured that the day you choose to follow Jesus wholeheartedly will be the day you see what true life is all about.

Called to Be the Light and to Surrender

Life is more than just growing a family and gaining finances to maintain your life. God wants to use you to impact the world and show His glorious ways.

> You are the light of the world. A town built on a hill cannot be hidden. Neither do people light a lamp and put it under a bowl. Instead they put it on its stand, and it gives light to everyone in the house. In the same way, let your light shine before others, that they may see your good deeds and glorify your Father in heaven.
>
> Matthew 5:14–16 (NIV)

You were created to be the light of the world. Your world may look different in every season. For a season, your world could be your family, workplace, city, nation, or world. Whatever your world may be, choose to be the light of the world and give your life to follow Jesus.

The key to living a satisfied life is to live the life that Jesus has called you to live. Our own version of our lives will never be as satisfying as His. Jesus said, "My food…is to do the will of him who sent me and to finish his work" (John 4:34 NIV). Jesus knew that true satisfaction comes from doing the will of God.

Doing the will of God requires us to die to our flesh and desires. There is no way we can follow Jesus if we are still seeking to fulfill our own desires and wants. Choosing Jesus is choosing to give ourselves to Him. It is a life of daily surrender. Jesus tells us, "Whoever wants to be my disciple must deny themselves and take up their cross daily and follow me" (Luke 9:23 NIV).

It sounds harsh to deny ourselves, but it's in *denying ourselves that we truly save ourselves.* Our heart is deceitful, and we don't know what is best for us. By nature, we are all prone to sin because we were born into sin.

But Jesus died and rose again to take upon Himself our sins so we can be redeemed and live our lives to the fullest. We now have the Holy Spirit who lives inside us and empowers us to walk in righteousness. May God open our eyes to see His law as wonderful (Psalm 119:18).

Every disciple in the Bible left everything to follow Jesus. We are all called to be disciples, so we, too, must leave our will and take on the will of God.

The secret of a satisfied life is giving ourselves to Jesus. *Absolute satisfaction is found in absolute surrender to Jesus.*

I am here today because of the many decisions I made to lay my own plans down for God's plans. I wouldn't be here today if it wasn't for the guidance of Jesus.

Following Jesus means surrendering things you never expected to surrender. I never expected to let go of my desire to pursue a master's degree or even to let go of my previous relationship. But for everything God asked me to let go of, He replaced them with something better.

Don't Wait for Fear to Disappear

Don't wait until your fears are completely gone to obey God. If I had waited for my fears to leave before taking a step of faith, I would have never obeyed God.

If you keep waiting for your fears to disappear, you will never step into God's Promised Land for your life. Adventuring with God will require you to take steps of faith, *even when you still have fear.*

Think about the time you went on a roller coaster. There's always that slight fear in your stomach that you have to deal with, but you keep going because you know you will be safe and the fun will be well worth it.

We need to see our adventures with God in a similar way and remember that the fear we have is not real and what is to come will be well worth it. *God has never failed and will never fail.*

Facing your fears will require you to move forward even when you're afraid. You will never experience the thrill of sky-diving if you wait for your fear of jumping off an airplane to leave. There's always going to be that slight fear deep in your heart, but you just have to go for it.

Take that leap of faith. Jump, and take that risk. Know that God is with you and that His plans for your life are always the best.

If I had waited for my fear of singleness to leave before breaking up with my ex-boyfriend, I never would have obeyed God. It was three months later that my fear of singleness completely left. If I had waited for all my fears to leave, I would have stayed in the wrong relationship.

I once heard someone say, "As long as you're in the wrong relationship, you will never be in the right relationship."

Don't allow fear to stop you from being with the one God has for you. Your fears will eventually leave, but sometimes it means we first have to take a leap of faith in order for the fear to leave.

Use the Word of God

For three months after my breakup, I had to be intentional with clinging to the Word of God. When fear crept in, I renewed my mind with the truth that He is faithful and that He always knows best.

Don't take even a moment to think about the past or your fears because you are only giving the enemy a foothold when you do. Respond to the fearful thoughts with God's Word, and don't converse with the enemy any longer. Thinking about your fears is you conversing with the enemy. We must respond to the enemy with God's Word and stand firm without considering what the enemy has to say.

The difference between Eve's response to the enemy in Genesis 3 and Jesus's response to the enemy in Matthew 4 is that Eve responded with God's words but still considered what the enemy had to say. Jesus, on the other hand, spoke the Word of God so the enemy would depart. Jesus had no intention of conversing with the enemy or considering his ways. Jesus had His complete trust in the validity and goodness of God's Word.

Jesus responded this way to the enemy's last temptation: "Away from me, Satan! For it is written: 'Worship the Lord your God, and serve him only'" (Matthew 4:10 NIV).

Don't tolerate the temptations of the enemy or dwell on the past. In the midst of our wilderness, we must focus our attention on *what is to come.* Our fears and past will only hold us back from walking in God's beautiful plans for our lives.

Remember, *God's Word propels us forward, and our fears hold us back.*

Your Obedience Matters

The disciples said to Jesus, "Increase our faith!" (Luke 17:5 NIV). Jesus replied, "If you have faith as small as a mustard seed, you can say to this mulberry tree, 'Be uprooted and planted in the sea,' and it will obey you" (Luke 17:6 NIV).

God was reminding the disciples that they didn't need more faith; they needed to obey God with the *little faith* they had.

Our obedience with just a little faith has the power to move mountains and see the impossible become possible.

Jesus then says, "So you also, when you have done everything you were told to do, should say, 'We are unworthy servants; we have only done our duty'" (Luke 17:10 NIV). That shows that Jesus simply wants our obedience. The great miracles that will happen in our lives will simply come from our obedience to Jesus.

All He asks us to do is obey Him, and we can watch Him do the rest. It's His job to transform our hearts and take us where we need to be. We just have to say yes and follow Him despite what we feel.

God loves you and has the best in store for you. This is the season when God wants to transform you from the inside out. Old mindsets and bondages that once held you captive are now being broken as you take this step of obedience to Jesus.

Keep moving forward, and don't look back. Remember that *what is to come is better than what was.* As long as you keep looking back, you will not be able to move forward in the new season and promises that God has for you.

The older generation of Israelites missed their Promised Land because they held on to old mindsets. Their temporary struggles through the wilderness made them forget God's faithfulness. They complained and said this to Moses:

> If only we had died by the LORD's hand in Egypt! There we sat around pots of meat and ate all the food we wanted, but you have brought us out into this desert to starve this entire assembly to death.
>
> Exodus 16:3 (NIV)

The Israelites had lost their gratitude to God for releasing them from slavery under Pharaoh. God was faithful countless times along their journey and provided food and water, yet they forgot God time and time again.

When Moses went up on Mount Sinai, they built their own idol and worshiped that instead of God. Their hearts became far from God, and that caused them to miss their Promised Land.

God had clearly spoken and said to the Israelites, "I have promised to bring you up out of your misery in Egypt into the land of the Canaanites, Hittites, Amorites, Perizzites, Hivites and Jebusites—a land flowing with milk and honey"

(Exodus 3:17 NIV). The hard journey had made them forget that God was with them and that God had a beautiful promise for them.

Have you forgotten the God who also goes before you? Are you still holding on to the promises He has for your life? Will you still believe that He has the perfect spouse for you?

We must not forget the God who is with us when the journey gets hard. Press forward, and walk faithfully with the Lord, trusting that in His time He will deliver us to our own Promised Land. "Hope in the LORD and keep his way. He will exalt you to inherit the land" (Psalm 37:34 NIV).

I believe you are in a place where you know what you must do. The question now is this: *Will you do what must be done despite what you feel?* God's promises for your life are worth more than anything in this world. Remember that your present sufferings are not worth comparing to the glory that will be revealed through you (Romans 8:18).

Paul reminds us to keep moving toward our goal.

> Brothers and sisters, I do not consider myself yet to have taken hold of it. But one thing I do: Forgetting what is behind and straining toward what is ahead, I press on toward the goal to win the prize for which God has called me heavenward in Christ Jesus.
> Philippians 3:13–14 (NIV)

What do you need to forget from the past and leave behind in this season?

We can never move forward if we're looking back.

God warned Lot and his family to not look back as He was rescuing them from the destruction of the city of Sodom and Gomorrah. Lot's wife looked back, however, and became a pillar of salt (Genesis 19). God had plans to take Lot's wife to a new place for a better life, but she looked back and got destroyed.

The things He asks us to leave have the power to destroy the plans He has for our lives. God only asks us to forget what is behind because what is coming is greater than what we are leaving.

God may be asking you to let go of an old relationship or a past of drugs and lust. Whatever it may be, let it go, and press forward to the new season He has for you.

> And no one puts new wine into old wine-skins. For the old skins would burst from the pressure, spilling the wine and ruining the skins. New wine is stored in new wineskins so that both are preserved.
>
> Matthew 9:17 (NLT)

What Jesus was saying in this verse is that He can't do the new things in our lives when we have our old mindsets. God wants to transform you into a new person. Your new person in Christ cannot keep your old desires and mindsets.

Just as oil and water don't mix, so our old mindsets can't mix with our new mindsets in Christ.

> Forget the former things;
>   do not dwell on the past.
> See, I am doing a new thing!
>   Now it springs up; do you not perceive it?
> I am making a way in the wilderness
>   and streams in the wasteland.
>
> Isaiah 43:18–19 (NIV)

God is longing to do a new thing in your life. He wants to take your broken heart, fill it with rivers of living water, and show you what true joy is in Him.

The path of God will not always be the easiest path, but it will be the most rewarding path you could ever take. God longs to take you on an adventure where you get to see His goodness and faithfulness beyond what you could ever imagine. *Are you ready to adventure with God?*

God help me continue to look forward and not backward. Give me the strength to persevere and trust in You. What's coming is not worth losing by going back to what You have called me to leave behind.

Living in Freedom

We all long for freedom, but are we truly living a life of freedom? Having freedom and living in freedom are two different things.

Having freedom means we are given free will. Living in freedom means we are actually living out the free will given to us. That means we are able to make choices without anything hindering us.

Here are some questions to ask yourself to see if you are living in freedom:

1. Do I have fears or addictions that stop me from doing what I believe is right?
2. Am I consistently having thoughts that don't align with who I am in Christ?
3. Am I making decisions based on what others want me to do more than what I want to do?
4. Am I constantly displaying emotions that are not aligned with the fruits of the spirit, which are love, joy, peace, forbearance, kindness, goodness, faithfulness, gentleness, and self-control? (Galatians 5:22–23).

If your answer is yes to any of the questions above, then you are not living in the *full* freedom that Christ came to give you. The key to living in true freedom is to first know the truth. "Then you will know the truth, and the truth will set you free" (John 8:32 NIV).

Once we know God's truth, we must *believe it and live it out*. The fruit of freedom comes as we obey God. We will never find true freedom from simply knowing the truth. Knowledge of God's Word must then be lived out in order for us to see its results. "But be doers of the word, and not hearers only, deceiving yourselves" (James 1:22 NKJV).

The moment I realized I couldn't break up with my boyfriend despite knowing he wasn't the right one for me was the moment I realized I wasn't living out the true freedom that Christ died to give me. My will was bound by my fear of singleness and insecurity.

I knew deep inside that my boyfriend wouldn't fit in the life God was calling me to, yet I couldn't obey God and let him go. It was at that moment that I realized I was bound by fear that had to be broken.

We may be given the choice to make our own decisions, but are we bound by fears or addictions? If there is anything holding us back from doing what is right, we are not living out the freedom Christ came to give us. We can try to come up with reasons to justify our actions, but deep inside, we're just afraid.

I had to confess that fear was holding me back. It was when I confessed my fears that God was able to break my fears.

"If we confess our sins, he is faithful and just and will forgive us our sins and purify us from all unrighteousness" (1 John 1:9 NIV). There is a condition to that verse—"if we confess our sins." We will never change until we first confess that we need to change. Once we confess to Jesus, He cleanses us with His blood and empowers us to live the Christlike life.

My last breakup was the hardest thing I ever had to do, but as I asked God for His strength and grace, He helped me through it. One reason breaking up with my boyfriend was hard was because I was already close to his parents—particularly his mom. I had feelings of guilt that made it even harder to break up with my boyfriend.

I prayed to God and told Him, "God, you know how hard this is. I know it's my own fault for prolonging this relationship, but I ask You to help me be bold to do what I have to do. I ask that You help soften his mom's heart to be okay with this breakup."

To my surprise, the next day after praying this prayer, his mom texted me and encouraged me to follow my heart, even if it meant breaking up with her son. God's grace is able to help us through even the toughest decisions we have to make. Ask God, and He will help you. Change your *I can't* to *I can by the grace of God.* God's grace empowers us to live the life He created us to live—to live holy and do His will. "Continue to work out your salvation with fear and trembling, for it is God who works in you to will and to act in order to fulfill his good purpose" (Philippians 2:12–13 NIV).

Temptations will come, but we have been equipped through the power of Christ and His Word to live a victorious life.

Your Freedom Was Meant to Set Others Free

Before we can set others free, we must first be set free.

The Spirit of the Sovereign LORD is on me,
because the LORD has anointed me
to proclaim good news to the poor.

He has sent me to bind up the brokenhearted,
to proclaim freedom for the captives
and release from darkness for the prisoners.
Isaiah 61:1 (NIV)

God longs to use you to set others free. Every struggle and sin you've had to overcome was meant to help others overcome. Proclaim Isaiah 61:1 over your own life. Ask God to give you supernatural strength to release you from every bondage that has kept you from living in His full freedom.

I now can help others live a pure life because I have lived a pure life. I have the anointing to help others let go of wrong relationships and enter into right ones because I had the courage to let go of past wrong relationships.

There have been many times in the past when I have contemplated whether obeying God would be worth it. I knew at the time that I could never help others let go of wrong relationships or leave the impure life if I didn't do it myself. I would have been a hypocrite, but because I passed the test and overcame my strongholds, I now get to help others break their strongholds.

God has a mighty plan for your life. Every struggle you have faced was meant to propel you to help others. Step into the freedom and power God has destined you for. Ephesians 6:10 reminds us to be strong in the Lord and in His mighty power. The next verse tells us to put on the full armor of God so we can take our stand against the devil's schemes.

The devil wants to keep you bound from the great and unimaginable things God has in store for you. The enemy is a deceiver and will whisper in your ear that you're not missing out on anything when he knows that you're missing out on a life of full joy and freedom.

Walking in the Freedom of Christ

Anyone can be set free through Christ when they confess their sins, ask God for forgiveness, and believe Him as their Lord and Savior. John 8:36 (NIV) says, "So if the Son sets you free, you will be free indeed." Christ has the power to set you free. His Word is your armor to stand your ground for the rest of the days to come.

There are three steps to walking in the freedom of Christ:

1. Acknowledge what is keeping you bound.
2. Confess it to Jesus.
3. Live out the truth.

Acknowledge What Is Keeping You Bound

The Holy Spirit has the power to show us our weaknesses. Invite Him to inspect your heart and show you areas where there may be anxiety or anything that brings offense to Him.

> Search me, God, and know my heart;
>> test me and know my anxious thoughts.
> See if there is any offensive way in me,
>> and lead me in the way everlasting.
>> Psalm 139:23–24 (NIV)

There have been times when I did not realize I had sin in my heart. It wasn't until I invited the Holy Spirit to inspect me and show me areas that were bringing disunity between me and God that I recognized my own sin. There have also been times when I needed God to show me the roots of my anxiety.

Allow the Holy Spirit to help you acknowledge the sins that are keeping you bound. Make this your prayer: *Holy Spirit, I ask that You show me the depths of my heart. Reveal to me any anxiety I may have and anything else that brings offense to You. Show me the root of it all, and remove it from me with Your truth. Show me the way to a life full of Your freedom and joy.*

Confess It to Jesus

Once we have identified the source of our bondage, we must then confess it to Jesus. We must confess our sins in order for Jesus to forgive us and purify us from all unrighteousness (1 John 1:9).

We can ask Jesus—our Great Physician—to examine us. He points out our unhealthy roots and removes them with His truth. He has the power to wash away all the stains of our sins and wrongful thinking. Whether it is anxiety, anger, or lust you are dealing with, Jesus has the power to purify your heart.

Make this your prayer: *Jesus, I confess that I struggle with* _____. *I give this to You and ask that You remove it and wash me clean. I ask that You create in me a pure heart. Help me walk faithfully before You and have a heart that is pleasing in Your sight. I thank You that You make me new in You.*

Live Out the Truth

We must live out the truth *despite what we feel*. The reason I say "despite what we feel" is because there may be moments when we don't feel like living out the truth. Some people experience immediate change the moment they come to Jesus, while for others, it may be a process.

I've heard stories of people who were drug addicts getting radically changed by Jesus and losing the addiction the moment they came to Him. However, I have also heard stories of people who stopped using drugs but still struggled with the temptation for months. The results of both are the same—*they found freedom.* One just had a longer process to *complete* their freedom.

Despite what we feel, we must choose to live out the truth. God will never treat us like robots. He will always give us a choice to walk in truth. That is why Paul said, "Walk by the Spirit, and you will not gratify the desires of the flesh" (Galatians 5:16 NIV). As we deny our flesh and give ourselves to Jesus, He will transform us and change our hearts. The power to be set free comes from Jesus alone. *Our job is to offer ourselves as a living sacrifice. Jesus's job is to transform us.*

> Offer your bodies as a living sacrifice... Do not conform to the pattern of this world, but be transformed by the renewing of your mind. Then you will be able to test and approve what God's will is—his good, pleasing and perfect will.
>
> Romans 12:1–2 (NIV)

Only when we choose to obey God will we see His perfect will in our lives. Surrendering our lives to Jesus is the key to living a life of true freedom. We must be willing to be set free in order for Him to set us free.

I didn't wait for God to remove my fear of singleness before obeying Him in breaking up with my ex-boyfriend.

I obeyed despite having the fear in my heart. As I walked in obedience, the fear completely left me after three months.

Your process will look different than mine, but you can trust that the final result will be the same. You will walk in true freedom and be transformed.

> *Jesus, I surrender and give my life to You. I choose to deny my own desires to pick up Yours. I ask that You change my heart and transform me from the inside out. I don't know what the future holds, but I do trust that You know what is best for me. Strengthen me day by day as I walk out Your will in my life.*

Don't Rush—Wait for the Right One

You've probably heard this many times from loved ones: "Don't rush getting into a relationship. You're still young, and there will still be someone for you." I heard that a million times from my own mom. My worry was never that someone wouldn't want to be with me. I was worried that I wouldn't find someone I would want to be with. Another fear I had was not finding someone I could be comfortable with, thinking that my ex was going to be the only person I could be myself with.

But what I've learned that I want to tell you today is that *not rushing* is the best thing you could ever do. *Wait for the right one.* Don't think about going back to the one God told you to break up with, and don't rush into another relationship without God's confirmation. Once the right person comes into your life, only then can you rush into marriage—if God permits it!

I never thought I would date for only one year and then get married. I always saw myself dating someone for at least two to three years before getting married, but God had other plans.

I met my husband, and within one year, we got married. He was the first man I waited for God to confirm to be my husband before officially being in a relationship. After

God confirmed it in various ways, we didn't wait for years to get married. We got pre-marital counseling and prepared to get married later that year.

We certainly didn't prolong our dating season, but we didn't rush getting into a relationship either. I want to encourage you not to rush into a relationship with someone. Wait for God to finish the process He wants to teach you as you wait for the right person.

You might be in my situation where God already showed me the one who would be my husband. However, in the first three months of receiving that confirmation, God told me He still wanted me to be single. He was calling me to be in my cocoon because He was still in the process of molding me into the woman He wanted me to be.

We have to make sure we don't rush into a relationship because God has shown us the right person or because it's just our desire to be in a relationship. If God is still calling you in your cocoon season, *stay there*. He wants to teach you *perseverance, reliance, and satisfaction* in Him. It is the season when He wants to teach you what it means to truly trust in Him. We can easily say we trust God, but the truth shows when we come to the place where God makes a request and waits to see if we will obey or not.

If there is any hesitancy to obey God or wait to get into a relationship, it means we haven't fully trusted God. *Our fears and desires are still stronger than our desire to follow Jesus.*

If we want to truly be His disciple and see His perfect will in our lives, we must learn to *trust and obey*. Here's what Jesus said:

> If anyone comes to me and does not hate father and mother, wife and children, broth-
> ers and sisters—yes, even their own life—

such a person cannot be my disciple. And whoever does not carry their cross and follow me cannot be my disciple.

Luke 14:26–27 (NIV)

This may sound harsh, but what Jesus is saying is that we cannot have any greater lovers than Him. Of course, Jesus doesn't tell us to neglect our families and spouses, but He does tell us *to love Him more* than we love them. He asks us to love Him more than our own desires.

It's when we truly come to a place of surrender that we find the utmost joy in our lives. We tend to think we know what's best for our lives, but only Jesus knows. We can try to make excuses so our disobedience sounds appealing and godly, but if what we are doing isn't what God says to do, *it is not* godly at all.

For the longest time I tried giving God reasons why staying with my ex-boyfriend was a good thing to do. I said I could help him have a closer relationship with God and that we could serve God together. Ultimately, I had to face the reality that *it just wasn't God's will.* God opened my eyes to see that He cared more about *my obedience than my sacrifice.*

Maybe you're at a place where you know God has asked you to let go of someone, but you've given Him reasons why you shouldn't. Maybe you have broken up the relationship *but not fully broken it up.* What I mean is, you're not officially together, but you're still *unofficially together.* You're still messaging the other person and helping him or her through personal struggles. That person is still the first one you go to for comfort and advice.

If you're in that position, you have to admit that you haven't fully obeyed God and let go of that person. Taking down a relationship status and not using the words *I love you* doesn't mean you have let that person go. You may still be *emotionally attached.*

I've done this very thing. I broke up with my boy-friend, but we were still unofficially together. We texted each other every day and kept up with one another's lives. In two months, we were together again.

If we don't cut off communications with the person we break up with, the cycle will keep occurring. You'll realize that God was right, and then you'll break up with that per-son again. Over time, things will be going well, you'll get back together, and you will find yourself back to where you were—convicted and realizing the relationship won't work.

This happened to me twice in my previous relationship. I eventually had to realize that if I continued in this relation-ship, I would never experience God's best for my life. The cycle would only continue, and getting married would be ever so burdensome.

I want to save you from headaches and pain by helping you walk in the path of joy. God promises us that He will lead us to the right paths and that in His presence comes joy (Psalm 16:11). If we are not walking in God's path, we will not experience His joy, which comes when we are in His presence. And dwelling in His presence requires us to walk with God.

You have the opportunity to walk with God and realign your life with Him. It's never too late to get your life right with God. I spent six years in two wrong relationships, but God was still faithful to bring my husband, Michael, into my life at the right time.

You have a God who is able to redeem the times. He is your redeemer. "I am the LORD your God, who teaches you to benefit, who leads you in the way you should go" (Isaiah 48:17 NASB).

God guides us for *our benefit*. This must be ingrained in our hearts if we are to obey God. If God says wait, then wait. If God says not that person, then stop pursuing that person.

If you see a red light, what happens when you keep going? You crash. I love sharing this analogy. The same thing happens when you don't stop when God shows you a red light in a relationship you may be pursuing. If you keep pursuing a relationship when God has shown you many red lights, you are bound to crash.

You will have complete peace when you meet the right person God has for you. You won't find yourself compromising with God's truth. You will be closer to God, and you will have joy because your relationship with the other person shows God's presence through holiness.

God has the right spouse for you in mind. He knows the desires of your heart. Trust in His timing. He makes everything beautiful in its time (Ecclesiastes 3:11).

Make a list of declarations of God's truth and promises. Then declare them over yourself every day. Here are some declarations I wrote for myself during my single season:

- God has a beautiful plan and future for me.
- Don't settle for less than God's best.
- My season of loneliness ends now.
- I am beautiful and wanted.
- I am fearfully and wonderfully made.
- God won't delay in doing His part, but I must not delay in doing my part.

Write down verses that speak to you in this season, and allow them to be the foundation you stand on. This was my go-to verse during my single season:

Do not throw away your confidence; it will be richly rewarded. You need to persevere so that when you have done the will of God, you will receive what he has promised.

Hebrews 10:35–36 (NIV)

It's when we persevere in what God has told us to do that we will see His blessings in the perfect time. There were many times when I was tempted to go back to my ex, but in those moments, I held on to Hebrews 10:35–36. I reminded myself that as I persevere in obeying what God has told me, I will see His reward in the right time.

Now I can say I have received my reward for obeying. It is my husband, Michael.

You will have different verses to hold on to in each season. Find the right verse that God wants you to hold on to in this season.

I remind myself often that God won't delay in doing His part, but I must not delay in doing my part. It reminds me that as long as I disobey, I am delaying God's promise from coming to pass. "When you make a vow to God, do not delay to fulfill it" (Ecclesiastes 5:4 NIV).

Don't delay in doing what is right. God has plans for you that are greater than what you could ever imagine. He has the right spouse who will align with God's vision for you. He knows the right person who will love you and bring you the utmost joy. Don't rush. *Wait for the right one.*

Embracing the Single Status

My goal for this book is that when you finish reading it, you will *embrace your single status*. Many of us dread the thought of being single. As long as we focus on what we're missing out on, we will miss the joy of the blessings God has for us now. God wants us to embrace our single status. We need to shift our focus from what we're missing out on to what we get to experience now—*single but in a relationship with God.*

The only way to embrace your single status is to embrace your relationship with God. When your relationship with God is your priority, no other relationship will take away your relationship with God.

If your relationship with God is in jeopardy because of another relationship, it is most likely because your relationship with God isn't your priority. You've allowed another person in your life to cause you to move away from your relationship with God. My hope is that after reading this book, you will have the courage to let go and embrace your single status with Jesus.

This is your opportunity to learn to cling to the only relationship that will *never fail you*—your relationship with your heavenly Father. People can lie to you, but God can never lie to you. Unfaithfulness is not His nature. "God is not human, that he should lie" (Numbers 23:19 NIV).

As you embrace your single season, embrace Jesus. That is how He wants to show you His *tangible goodness*. He wants to show you that He's everything you need and that He longs to give you your desires. He only asks that you seek Him first, because when He comes first, everything else comes to pass. "Take delight in the LORD, and he will give you the desires of your heart" (Psalm 37:4 NIV).

It might sound selfish that God wants us before we can have our other desires, but His agenda is only to lead us to true fulfillment. He is the only foundation we can build on to live a life of fulfillment. *Jesus is the key to fulfillment.*

Yes, being married will bring you happiness. Yes, having money will bring you happiness. Yes, living your purpose will bring you happiness. But what all these things *can never bring you* is fulfillment. They bring happiness but *never fulfillment*.

Jesus must have first place in your heart. He must be your true fulfillment in order for everything else in your life to bring fulfillment. Our marriage can only last when Jesus is in the center. Money can't control and destruct us when Jesus is in the center. Our purpose will never be enough unless Jesus is in the center.

Fulfillment requires Jesus.

Marriage alone without Jesus won't fix our issues. Money and a purposeful life will never be enough. *Fulfillment is found in Christ.*

Jesus tells us, "I have come that they may have life, and have it to the full" (John 10:10 NIV). Jesus came to be the foundation of a life of fulfillment.

How do we experience this fulfillment? The first step is by *surrendering everything to Jesus*. We must surrender our whole lives and agendas to Him. Only Jesus can fill the void that nothing else in this world can ever fill.

We can never experience this fulfillment unless we make the choice to surrender to Jesus. That is why Jesus always comes at us with an invitation to follow Him. It is then our choice to accept or decline His invitation.

Accepting His invitation is accepting a life of fulfillment in Him. Declining His invitation is accepting a life of chasing after fulfillment but never arriving at fulfillment.

Fulfillment isn't a person or an achievement—it's Jesus.

I could go on and on about how the things of this world will never be enough. Everything will only leave us thirsty for more. Jesus is the only one who satisfies. *Only Jesus is enough.* Once you have Jesus, you have everything you need.

He is what will heal your broken heart.
He is where provision lies.
He is where success and identity are found.
He is where love is found.
He is everything you need.

Will you give Jesus your whole heart and make Him first above all? Will you allow Jesus to be King over your life and trust His timing over yours?

Make the most of your relationship with Jesus during your single season. You will miss out on intimacy with Him as long as you keep looking forward to another season of your life.

This is the time to build your own personal adventure and track record of His faithfulness.

This is the time you get to build a strong foundation for your marriage and family in the future.

This is the time you can adventure with Him with no restrictions.

This is your season to *fly like an eagle.*

Don't allow the enemy to rob you of your joy in this season. He wants you to be in fear and worry as each day goes by. He wants you to believe you're missing out on being in a relationship. Enjoy each day, and know that God is faithful to bring the right spouse to you.

It's not worth settling for someone God does not want you to be with. The enemy will try to tempt you to settle for someone God hasn't chosen for you so you will never experience God's full plan for your life. The enemy's goal is to steal your opportunities to see God move in your life, kill your soul in the process, and destroy your life forever by being apart from God.

That was the enemy's plan since the beginning with Adam and Eve. He tried to point out an emptiness in Eve by telling her that if she ate from the tree of the knowledge of good and evil, she would be like God (Genesis 3:5). The enemy was telling Eve that she was missing out on something when really she wasn't. The enemy knew she had everything in her union with God, but he was successful at deceiving her.

Eve ended up eating from the tree of the knowledge of good and evil in an attempt to gain wisdom. What she failed to realize was that she had everything she needed in God. She didn't need to gain wisdom because *she had access* to the wisdom of God through her *relationship with God*.

We have to understand that our relationship with God brings us everything we need. That is why the enemy's goal is to separate us from God by leading us on paths that lead us away from Him.

The enemy's intention in making Adam and Eve sin was to separate them from God, which is exactly what happened. God had to cast them from the Garden of Eden, and they lost access to the kingdom of God.

The enemy will use sin (disobedience and unholiness to God) to separate us from God. His goal is to break our relationship with God. In moments of temptation, we must remember that *nothing* is worth being separated from God.

There are many who are single but are not truly embracing the season with joy and fulfillment. Many have turned to dating to remove their loneliness, to sex outside of marriage to fill their lack of intimacy, and to wrong relationships to remove their fear.

Do these things work? *Sadly, no.* Everything we pursue in hopes of bringing us closer to fulfillment only takes us further away from it. As we seek things outside of God, we create a deeper void in our hearts that causes us to want more.

Whether it's pornography, one-night stands, or relationships that God never meant for us to have, they leave us *emptier.* It creates a vicious cycle—pursuing what we believe will fulfill us, but it only leaves us emptier.

Only Jesus can fill us with everlasting joy and fulfillment. Jesus *freely gives* because He loves us.

Will you embrace Jesus as you embrace your single season?

We have to embrace Jesus before we can truly embrace our single season. The revelation of His love is what will sustain us. Yes, marriage is in God's heart, but we don't have to settle for less than God's best in order to fill a void. We can wait for the right one and enjoy our future marriage *to the fullest.*

We don't have to fall into the enemy's trap of disobeying God in order to gain our desires. God said He would give us the desires of our heart *as we desire Him.* He already sent Jesus to die on the cross for us so we could have everything Adam and Eve lost. He has now redeemed us through the blood of Jesus and has given us access to Him once again.

God now lives and makes His home in those who obey Him. "Anyone who loves me will obey my teaching. My Father will love them, and we will come to them and make our home with them" (John 14:23 NIV).

Nothing in this world is worth being separated from your relationship with Jesus. Embrace the season God has called you to. Embrace singleness as you embrace Jesus.

If you could have a life where you got to—

- live out the dreams you've always had in your heart;
- marry someone you love and are attracted to and who will support you;
- live each day with joy and peace, knowing you're in God's will;
- see God's miraculous hand craft your life story;
- partner with God to transform the world;
- be with Jesus for eternity,
  —would you choose that life?

I'm sure your answer is yes. The good news is that you have the opportunity to live this life. It isn't an unattainable dream life. It is offered to those who are willing to *walk a life of following Jesus.*

It is the life Jesus speaks of when He says He has come to give us life *to the fullest.*

As you embrace your single season with the Lord, you get to live life to the fullest. There is no peace unless you are living in the will of God. When you are in His will, you are guaranteed a *victorious end to your story.*

Always hold on to your relationship with God. Embrace it. Nourish it. Live it out.

Will you give Jesus your complete yes and let go of everything else that hinders your relationship with Him?

I'd like to end this book with a prayer for you to declare over yourself.

Jesus, from this day forward, I choose to lay down every part of my life for You and follow You wherever You lead me. I lay down my fears and pick up faith to walk with You. I will no longer tolerate the lies of the enemy but will walk according to Your Word. I make you my Savior, the one I long to live for. I let go of any relationships You don't want me to have. I choose this day to embark on my single season with boldness and faith and believe that You have the best spouse in store for me. I dedicate my life to You, Jesus.

God wants you to know that He sees you and knows you. Rest in the truth that your heavenly Father knows your needs. You never have to worry if God is making a mistake. He never makes mistakes, and you can trust His judgment. He is a good Father and will always lead you to life to the fullest.

This is the time to embrace your single season. *Will you say yes to being single but in a relationship with God?*

Epilogue

Thank you for reading this book. I pray that my story and the revelations in this book have helped you embrace your single season with God.

Check out my website, GabrielleSantiago.org/single-book, to get more resources to help you in your walk with God during your single season.

I'd also love to hear how this book has helped you. Share your story and testimony at gaby@livingrevelations.com.

About the Author

Gabrielle Santiago is the founder of Living Revelations Ministries where she helps others find God real in everyday life through blogs, podcasts, media, and Bible studies. Her writings have reached thousands of people worldwide. Her heart is to know Jesus more and make Him known. Her passion is to awaken a generation to follow Jesus into their God-given purpose.

You can listen to her podcasts on Apple or Spotify: Living Revelations.

Connect with her on her personal and ministry Instagram account:

Personal: Instagram.com/gabytsanti
Ministry: Instagram.com/livingrevelations
Subscribe to her podcasts and blogs at LivingRevelations.com.

CPSIA information can be obtained
at www.ICGtesting.com
Printed in the USA
BVHW030331180621
609823BV00004B/573